EXPLORING ENCRYPTION AND POTENTIAL MECHANISMS FOR AUTHORIZED GOVERNMENT ACCESS TO PLAINTEXT

Proceedings of a Workshop

Anne Johnson, Emily Grumbling, and Jon Eisenberg, *Rapporteurs*

Computer Science and Telecommunications Board

Division on Engineering and Physical Sciences

The National Academies of
SCIENCES • ENGINEERING • MEDICINE

THE NATIONAL ACADEMIES PRESS
Washington, DC
www.nap.edu

THE NATIONAL ACADEMIES PRESS   **500 Fifth Street, NW**   **Washington, DC 20001**

This activity was supported by the Office of the Director of National Intelligence, under Contract No. 2014-14041100003-010. Any opinions, findings, conclusions, or recommendations expressed in this publication do not necessarily reflect the views of any organization or agency that provided support for the project.

International Standard Book Number-13: 978-0-309-44740-9
International Standard Book Number-10: 0-309-44740-2
Digital Object Identifier: 10.17226/23593

Copies of this publication are available for sale from the National Academies Press, 500 Fifth Street, NW, Keck 360, Washington, DC 20001; (800) 624-6242 or (202) 334-3313; http://www.nap.edu.

Copyright 2016 by the National Academy of Sciences. All rights reserved.

Printed in the United States of America.

Suggested citation: National Academies of Sciences, Engineering, and Medicine, 2016. *Exploring Encryption and Potential Mechanisms for Authorized Government Access to Plaintext: Proceedings of a Workshop*. Washington, DC: The National Academies Press. doi: 10.17226/23593.

The National Academies of
SCIENCES · ENGINEERING · MEDICINE

The **National Academy of Sciences** was established in 1863 by an Act of Congress, signed by President Lincoln, as a private, nongovernmental institution to advise the nation on issues related to science and technology. Members are elected by their peers for outstanding contributions to research. Dr. Marcia McNutt is president.

The **National Academy of Engineering** was established in 1964 under the charter of the National Academy of Sciences to bring the practices of engineering to advising the nation. Members are elected by their peers for extraordinary contributions to engineering. Dr. C. D. Mote, Jr., is president.

The **National Academy of Medicine** (formerly the Institute of Medicine) was established in 1970 under the charter of the National Academy of Sciences to advise the nation on medical and health issues. Members are elected by their peers for distinguished contributions to medicine and health. Dr. Victor J. Dzau is president.

The three Academies work together as the **National Academies of Sciences, Engineering, and Medicine** to provide independent, objective analysis and advice to the nation and conduct other activities to solve complex problems and inform public policy decisions. The Academies also encourage education and research, recognize outstanding contributions to knowledge, and increase public understanding in matters of science, engineering, and medicine.

Learn more about the National Academies of Sciences, Engineering, and Medicine at **www.national-academies.org**.

The National Academies of
SCIENCES · ENGINEERING · MEDICINE

Reports document the evidence-based consensus of an authoring committee of experts. Reports typically include findings, conclusions, and recommendations based on information gathered by the committee and committee deliberations. Reports are peer reviewed and are approved by the National Academies of Sciences, Engineering, and Medicine.

Proceedings chronicle the presentations and discussions at a workshop, symposium, or other convening event. The statements and opinions contained in proceedings are those of the participants and have not been endorsed by other participants, the planning committee, or the National Academies of Sciences, Engineering, and Medicine.

For information about other products and activities of the Academies, please visit nationalacademies.org/whatwedo.

OTHER RECENT REPORTS OF THE COMPUTER SCIENCE AND TELECOMMUNICATIONS BOARD

Continuing Innovation in Information Technology: Workshop Report (2016)
Future Directions for NSF Advanced Computing Infrastructure to Support U.S. Science and Engineering in 2017-2020. (2016)
Privacy Research and Best Practices: Summary of a Workshop for the Intelligence Community (2016)

Bulk Collection of Signals Intelligence: Technical Options (2015)
Interim Report on 21st Century Cyber-Physical Systems Education (2015)
A Review of the Next Generation Air Transportation System: Implications and Importance of System Architecture (2015)
Telecommunications Research and Engineering at the Communications Technology Laboratory of the Department of Commerce: Meeting the Nation's Telecommunications Needs (2015)
Telecommunications Research and Engineering at the Institute for Telecommunication Sciences of the Department of Commerce: Meeting the Nation's Telecommunications Needs (2015)

At the Nexus of Cybersecurity and Public Policy: Some Basic Concepts and Issues (2014)
Emerging and Readily Available Technologies and National Security: A Framework for Addressing Ethical, Legal, and Societal Issues (2014)
Future Directions for NSF Advanced Computing Infrastructure to Support U.S. Science and Engineering in 2017-2020: An Interim Report (2014)
Interim Report of a Review of the Next Generation Air Transportation System Enterprise Architecture, Software, Safety, and Human Factors (2014)

Geotargeted Alerts and Warnings: Report of a Workshop on Current Knowledge and Research Gaps (2013)
Professionalizing the Nation's Cybersecurity Workforce? Criteria for Future Decision-Making (2013)
Public Response to Alerts and Warnings Using Social Media: Summary of a Workshop on Current Knowledge and Research Gaps (2013)

Computing Research for Sustainability (2012)
Continuing Innovation in Information Technology (2012)
The Safety Challenge and Promise of Automotive Electronics: Insights from Unintended Acceleration (2012, with the Board on Energy and Environmental Systems and the Transportation Research Board)

The Future of Computing Performance: Game Over or Next Level? (2011)
Public Response to Alerts and Warnings on Mobile Devices: Summary of a Workshop on Current Knowledge and Research Gaps (2011)
Strategies and Priorities for Information Technology at the Centers for Medicare and Medicaid Services (2011)
Wireless Technology Prospects and Policy Options (2011)

Achieving Effective Acquisition of Information Technology in the Department of Defense (2010)
Critical Code: Software Producibility for Defense (2010)
Improving State Voter Registration Databases (2010)
Proceedings of a Workshop on Deterring Cyberattacks: Informing Strategies and Developing Options for U.S. Policy (2010)
Toward Better Usability, Security, and Privacy of Information Technology: Report of a Workshop (2010)

Limited copies of CSTB reports are available free of charge from

Computer Science and Telecommunications Board
Keck Center of the National Academies of Sciences, Engineering, and Medicine
500 Fifth Street, NW, Washington, DC 20001
(202) 334-2605/cstb@nas.edu
www.cstb.org

PLANNING COMMITTEE FOR A WORKSHOP ON ENCRYPTION AND MECHANISMS FOR AUTHORIZED GOVERNMENT ACCESS TO PLAINTEXT

FRED H. CATE, Indiana University, *Chair*
DAN BONEH, Stanford University
FREDERICK R. CHANG, Southern Methodist University
ORIN KERR, George Washington University
SUSAN LANDAU, Worcester Polytechnic Institute

Staff

EMILY GRUMBLING, Program Officer, Computer Science and Telecommunications Board (CSTB)
JON EISENBERG, Director, CSTB
SHENAE BRADLEY, Administrative Assistant, CSTB
RENEE HAWKINS, Financial Manager, CSTB

COMPUTER SCIENCE AND TELECOMMUNICATIONS BOARD

FARNAM JAHANIAN, Carnegie Mellon University, *Chair*
LUIZ ANDRÉ BARROSO, Google, Inc.
STEVEN M. BELLOVIN, Columbia University
ROBERT F. BRAMMER, Brammer Technology, LLC
EDWARD FRANK, Brilliant Cloud & Lime Parity
SEYMOUR E. GOODMAN, Georgia Institute of Technology
LAURA HAAS, IBM Corporation
MARK HOROWITZ, Stanford University
MICHAEL KEARNS, University of Pennsylvania
ROBERT KRAUT, Carnegie Mellon University
SUSAN LANDAU, Worcester Polytechnic Institute
PETER LEE, Microsoft Corporation
DAVID E. LIDDLE, US Venture Partners
FRED B. SCHNEIDER, Cornell University
ROBERT F. SPROULL, University of Massachusetts, Amherst
JOHN STANKOVIC, University of Virginia
JOHN A. SWAINSON, Dell, Inc.
ERNEST J. WILSON, University of Southern California
KATHERINE YELICK, University of California, Berkeley

Staff

JON EISENBERG, Director
LYNETTE I. MILLETT, Associate Director

VIRGINIA BACON TALATI, Program Officer
SHENAE BRADLEY, Administrative Assistant
JANEL DEAR, Senior Program Assistant
EMILY GRUMBLING, Program Officer
RENEE HAWKINS, Financial and Administrative Manager
HERBERT S. LIN, Chief Scientist (emeritus)

For more information on CSTB, see its website http://www.cstb.org, write to CSTB at
National Academies of Sciences, Engineering, and Medicine, 500 Fifth Street, NW, Washington, DC 20001,
call (202) 334-2605, or email the CSTB at cstb@nas.edu.

Acknowledgment of Reviewers

This workshop proceedings has been reviewed in draft form by individuals chosen for their diverse perspectives and technical expertise. The purpose of this independent review is to provide candid and critical comments that will assist the institution in making its published workshop proceedings as sound as possible and to ensure that it meets institutional standards for objectivity, evidence, and responsiveness to the project's charge. The review comments and draft manuscript remain confidential to protect the integrity of the study process. We wish to thank the following individuals for their review of this workshop proceedings:

Dan Boneh, Stanford University,
Shafrira Goldwasser, Massachusetts Institute of Technology,
David S. Kris, Intellectual Ventures,
Brian A. LaMacchia, Microsoft Research,
Richard W. Littlehale, Tennessee Bureau of Investigation,
Kate Martin, Center for American Progress, and
Radia J. Perlman, EMC Corporation.

Although the reviewers listed above have provided many constructive comments and suggestions, they were not asked to endorse the views presented at the workshop, nor did they see the final draft of the workshop proceedings before its release. The review of this workshop proceedings was overseen by Samuel H. Fuller, Analog Devices, Inc., who was responsible for making certain that an independent examination of this proceedings was carried out in accordance with institutional procedures and that all review comments were carefully considered. Responsibility for the final content of this proceedings rests entirely with the authors and the institution.

Contents

1 OVERVIEW   1

2 WELCOME AND OPENING REMARKS   2

3 SESSION 1. THE CURRENT ENCRYPTION LANDSCAPE   3
    Introductory Remarks by Chris Inglis, 3
    Introductory Remarks by Patrick Ball, 4
    Introductory Remarks by James Baker, 6
    Discussion, 7
        Law Enforcement Capabilities and the Costs of Encryption, 7
        Do We Have More Data, or Less?, 8
        Which Tools Should We Entrust to the Government?, 8
        Dealing with Encryption in an International Context, 9
        Context Dependence of Government Needs and Obligations, 9
        Lessons from History, 10
        Practical Considerations, 11
        Final Remarks from Panelists, 11

4 SESSION 2. USE CASES AND THE FEASIBILITY OF SEGMENTING ENCRYPTION POLICIES   13
    Discussion, 14
        Institutional Context, 14
        Vertical Segmentation, 14
        Horizontal Segmentation, 15

5 SESSION 3. SECURITY RISKS OF ARCHITECTURES FOR ENABLING 17
   GOVERNMENT ACCESS TO PLAINTEXT
   Historical Context, 17
      Crypto War I, 17
      Crypto War II and the Cybersecurity Crisis, 18
      Fundamentals of the Current Cybersecurity Landscape, 19
      Exceptional Access: Considerations and Challenges, 19
   Discussion, 20
      Part 1: Issues and Context, 20
         Security Trade-offs, 20
         The Law Enforcement Context, 21
         The Industry Context, 22
         The Internet of Things, 23
      Part 2: Exploring Solutions, 24
         Requirements for an Exceptional Access System, 24
         Exploring a "k out of n" Solution, 25
         The Role of Hardware, 27
         The Feasibility of Segmenting by User, 28
         The Government's Technical Resources: Lawful Hacking and Other Considerations, 28
         Building a More Productive Conversation, 30

6 SESSION 4. TECHNICAL AND POLICY MITIGATIONS FOR INACCESSIBLE PLAINTEXT 31
   The Threat of Cybercrime, 31
   Trends in Wiretapping, 32
   Lawful Hacking, 33
   The Role of Metadata, 34
   The Internet of Things, 34
   Potential Solutions, 34
   Discussion, 35
      Unintended Outcomes and the Balance Between Legal and Technical Protections, 35
      Exploring Divergent Perspectives on Metadata, 36
      Phone-Based Authentication: Strengths and Weaknesses, 37
      The Government's Responsibilities When Vulnerabilities Are Exposed, 38

7 WRAP-UP SESSION 39
   Costs of Exceptional Access, 39
   Practical Considerations, 40
   Global Dimensions of Encryption and Access Mechanisms, 41
   Meeting Law Enforcement Needs, 42
   Disclosure of Vulnerabilities, 43
   The Use of Metadata, 43
   Closing Remarks from the Workshop Chair: Technology as Part of a System, 44

APPENDIXES

A Workshop Statement of Task 49
B Workshop Agenda 50
C Biographical Sketches of Workshop Planning Committee and Staff 52
D Biographical Sketches of Invited Workshop Participants 55
E Acronyms and Abbreviations 60

1

Overview

The Workshop on Encryption and Mechanisms for Authorized Government Access to Plaintext was convened on June 23-24, 2016, in Washington, D.C., under the auspices of the Computer Science and Telecommunications Board of the National Academies of Sciences, Engineering, and Medicine. The workshop was sponsored by the Office of the Director of National Intelligence (ODNI).

The workshop was planned by an appointed planning committee and by Academies' staff (Appendix C). Invited participants (Appendix D) along with the planning committee were convened to discuss, in an objective and technically rigorous way, potential encryption strategies that would enable access to plaintext information by law enforcement or national security agencies with appropriate authority. Appendix A provides the full statement of task, and Appendix B provides the agenda for the workshop. Speakers were invited to participate based on their own knowledge and experience; the views expressed at the workshop do not necessarily reflect the official views of their organizations. Although the focus of the workshop was on technical issues, several speakers were invited specifically to provide thoughts on the broader policy context, and discussion about the topics of encryption and authorized exceptional analysis frequently addressed open policy questions as well as technical issues. Moreover, as the proceedings of a single workshop, this summary does not cover the full landscape of technological solutions or legal and policy considerations.

The workshop was organized as follows. Opening remarks were delivered by Fred H. Cate, workshop planning committee chair. An introductory panel addressed the current encryption landscape, providing context for the three subsequent sessions, each introduced by a 30-minute presentation followed by a moderated discussion among the planning committee and invited participants. The workshop concluded with a final wrap-up session, during which invited participants, a few members of the audience, and members of the planning committee shared final points and reflections from the workshop.

These proceedings have been prepared by the workshop rapporteurs as a factual summary of what occurred at the workshop. The planning committee's role was limited to planning and convening the workshop. The views contained in the report are those of individual workshop participants and do not necessarily represent the views of their employers, the workshop participants as a whole, the planning committee, the Academies, the sponsor, or any other affiliated organizations.

The meeting was open to the public. These proceedings were created from the presenters' slides, notes, and a full transcript of the proceedings to serve as a public record of the workshop presentations and discussions. Workshop speakers were given an opportunity to review and correct the summaries of their remarks.

2

Welcome and Opening Remarks

The workshop opened with framing remarks delivered by Fred H. Cate, C. Ben Dutton Professor of Law at Indiana University Maurer School of Law and chair of the workshop planning committee. He began with an overview of the workshop's goals and parameters.

Recognizing that the topic of encryption and government access has engendered lively debate and that attendees hold diverse perspectives, Cate expressed his hope that the workshop could help to move the conversation forward by exploring the different and sometimes conflicting views on the technologies involved in encryption and mechanisms for obtaining access to plaintext. He emphasized that the workshop will not produce recommendations of any sort and does not aim to achieve consensus among attendees. He also clarified that the workshop is not intended to grapple with the wide range of values involved in considerations about government access to plaintext or to be a forum for evaluating how the country should proceed with regard to policy or other actions.

Cate summarized the workshop's purpose as elucidating the potential options in a technologically rigorous way and outlined the meeting's four focus areas:

1. The current encryption landscape,
2. Encryption use cases and the feasibility of segmenting encryption policies,
3. Security risks of architectures for enabling access to plaintext, and
4. Technical and policy mitigations for inaccessible plaintext.

Later in the workshop, Cate brought attendees' attention to a National Academies of Sciences, Engineering, and Medicine study currently under way titled "Law Enforcement and Intelligence Access to Plaintext Information in an Era of Widespread Strong Encryption: Options and Trade-offs," which is intended to dive deeper into many of the topics being discussed at the workshop. That study is slated for completion in 2017.

Cate acknowledged the workshop sponsor, the Office of the Director of National Intelligence, which requested the workshop in an effort to bring together a wide range of perspectives to advance the discussion in a neutral forum. He also expressed gratitude to the workshop organizers, including the planning committee members and Computer Science and Telecommunications Board staff members, who worked quickly to organize in a matter of weeks a high-caliber workshop that would typically have taken months to plan.

3

Session 1. The Current Encryption Landscape

The first session was moderated by Fred Cate and featured opening remarks from three panelists: Chris Inglis, Distinguished Visiting Professor in Cyber Security Studies, U.S. Naval Academy, and former deputy director of the National Security Agency (NSA); Patrick Ball, director of research at the Human Rights Data Analysis Group (HRDAG); and James Baker, general counsel for the Federal Bureau of Investigation (FBI). The speakers shared their perceptions of the encryption landscape today based on their diverse experiences. In particular,

- Inglis emphasized that any use of cryptography and potential systems for exceptional access must be based on well-defined goals and uses.
- Ball championed cryptography's importance in protecting human rights internationally and in the United States and offered a cautionary message about the threat of government abuses.
- Baker underscored the FBI's role as a servant of the American people and emphasized that while the increasing use of encryption has made investigations more difficult, the FBI does not intend to impose on the population any particular solution.

Following a brief introductory statement from each of the panelists, Cate moderated a general discussion covering many aspects of the debate over giving government actors exceptional access to plaintext from encrypted data.[1] Participants considered the differences when thinking about the problem from an international, federal, and state or local perspective; differing levels of trust in government and various perceptions of government's motivations for exceptional access; and the difference between the possible and the practical in terms of both technical capabilities and the decision-making framework.

INTRODUCTORY REMARKS BY CHRIS INGLIS

Chris Inglis retired from the Department of Defense in 2014 after more than 41 years of federal service, including 28 years at the NSA and seven and a half years as its senior civilian and deputy director. Noting that his

---

[1] Throughout this summary, as at the workshop, the term "plaintext" refers to data in its unencrypted form, "encryption" refers to the use of cryptographic algorithms to encode data so that it cannot be read by an unintended recipient, and "exceptional access" refers to situations where the government or another authorized party "needs and can obtain" the plaintext of encrypted data. (National Research Council, *Cryptography's Role in Securing the Information Society* (K.W. Dam and H.S. Lin, eds.), National Academy Press, Washington, D.C., 1996, p. 80.)

views are influenced by his time at the NSA but that he does not speak for the NSA, Inglis began by emphasizing that when designing encryption frameworks, one must consider how they will be used. Any system comprises both technology and doctrine (he defined the latter as the set of appropriate purposes for and uses of technology). That context, he said, must be a part of any discussion about access. He said the goals of encryption are best defined before the technology is built, instead of starting with the technology and then "bending it" to suit a particular application. Rather than being drawn into an unproductive conversation that pits individual expectations for privacy, security, or other aims against collective security objectives supported by exceptional government access, he advised drawing lessons from the marketplace; different companies have made starkly different choices about how their technology will be used and then designed their technology to suit those purposes. Apple, for example, could be read to support ubiquitous encryption with no possibility of exceptional access, even by the company itself. On the other hand, access to plaintext is vital to the Google's business prospects, and it has built exceptional access into communications streams under controlled, transparent conditions. Although those are two very different choices, they offer examples of how technology can be built to accommodate specific goals that are decided up front.

Inglis concluded his remarks by stating that there has never been a perfect encryption system; even when the math is correct, implementation is never perfect; as a result, encryption will never meet all expectations. This further underscores the importance of doctrine, which he finds as important as the encryption itself. In closing, Inglis expressed confidence that his fellow workshop participants would be able to create systems to meet whatever set of requirements were decided upon. While recognizing that the goal of the workshop is not to achieve consensus on what those expectations are, he said that setting out such groundwork is necessary for a truly thoughtful discussion about the merits of any particular implementation.

INTRODUCTORY REMARKS BY PATRICK BALL

Patrick Ball, director of research at the Human Rights Data Analysis Group has spent 25 years conducting data analysis on human rights violations committed by governments around the world. He also acknowledged colleagues he had surveyed for information and experiences to inform his remarks; these included colleagues from various organizations, among them the Electronic Frontier Foundation, Access Now, Human Rights Watch, the Center for Media Justice, and the Genentech Initiative.

Ball presented an overview of the technology landscape based on a 2016 survey by the Berkman Center[2] describing a range of encryption products, including file encryption; full-disk encryption; e-mail, messaging, and voice encryption; virtual private network solutions; and tools for digital signatures. Overall, one-third of these products were made in the United States, while the rest were made abroad. About two-thirds were commercial products and one-third was free and open source. Many, said Ball, were software libraries (rather than stand-alone encryption tools), which provide building blocks that make it "fairly easy" to build encryption into a software application. As an illustration, Ball described his own experience with the development of Martus, a free, open-source, secure tool designed to enable human rights workers to safely collect, encrypt, and store information that a government could view as threatening. Martus is one of many open-source encryption products available for human rights groups to use to protect activists from government violence and repression. In the context of the wide availability of encryption systems, Ball emphasized that it is impossible to prevent people or governments from using them. If a government "back door" were created for legal encryption schemes, smart criminals and terrorists would only be more incentivized to build and use illegal encryption systems that do not contain the back door. If the FBI were to break or otherwise gain access to legal encryption schemes, in his view, that would only provide access to information encrypted by less sophisticated criminals—and from the law-abiding world, as well.

Ball pointed to numerous groups around the world who use cryptography to shield their efforts from governments that might oppose them. Examples include journalists' associations in Egypt, Uganda, Rwanda, and Nicaragua; lesbian, gay, bisexual, and transgender groups in Jordan, Serbia, Morocco, and central and southern Africa; democracy activists in Ethiopia, Turkey, and Kyrgyzstan; human rights activists across east Africa,

---

[2] B. Schneier, K. Seidel, and S. Vijayakumar, 2016, "A Worldwide Survey of Encryption Products," Berkman Center Research Publication No. 2016-2, http://ssrn.com/abstract=2731160.

Cambodia, Tunisia, and Latin America; and environmental activists in India and Ecuador. The threats such groups fear most, he said, are their own local governments' military and police. He also noted that many of the encryption tools human rights groups use were funded by grants from the U.S. Department of State, underscoring the department's view that U.S. interests are served by supporting independent nongovernmental organizations that hold corrupt, often brutal, governments publicly accountable for their actions. Ball then briefly described examples from his own experiences using encryption in the course of human rights investigations abroad. In Guatemala, where Ball worked on and off for more than 20 years, human rights workers collected and analyzed information about the genocidal violence carried out against the Ixil people by José Efraín Rios Montt, Guatemala's president in 1982 and 1983, which involved the murder of some 100,000 civilians over 18 months. The evidence collected by Ball and others, stored in databases that were encrypted nightly to protect them against theft and use by government actors, was ultimately used in the 2013 trial in which General Rios was convicted of genocide and crimes against humanity. Ball noted that documents uncovered in the course of the investigation revealed that in the 1980s the Guatemalan National Police regularly exchanged information with the FBI, primarily about training, narcotics investigations, and suspects. For the National Police, "suspects" included human rights activists, student and labor leaders, and dissident professors, although the nature of the information provided to the National Police by the FBI is not known. Iraq, where several groups use Martus to protect data collected about human rights violations, provides another illustrative example. Ball has shared technology and training with Yezidi human rights groups to help them securely document violence against their community, which Ball described as "one of the strongest prima facie cases of genocide I know of in recent years." He noted that those collecting these data are concerned both about potential assassinations of witnesses and human rights workers by Daesh[3] and seizure of their data by agents of the Iraqi state for propaganda purposes.

Ball emphasized that encryption is necessary not only for human rights groups working abroad. He noted that government surveillance is also a significant concern for human rights and civil liberties groups working in the United States. He provided the example of Human Rights Watch, which uses secure telephony for cell phone calls where possible, end-to-end encrypted video conferencing, and two types of commercial encryption for internal e-mail. He also noted that journalists in the United States often use SecureDrop, an open-source "whistleblower submission system" to communicate securely with anonymous sources. This is essential, Ball believes, because a journalist's freedom to pursue stories can sometimes be at odds with government wishes, even in the United States. Ball pointed to moments in American history in which the government conducted surveillance of its people, including civil rights and antiwar activists such as Martin Luther King, Jr., Malcom X, and Muhammad Ali in the 1960s and individuals critical of U.S. policy in Central America in the 1980s. Today, the Black Lives Matter movement has drawn attention to disproportionate police violence committed against people of color. Ball noted that, while some of these police actions may be necessary, legal, or justified, the FBI does not record this information accurately or comprehensively. In his view, the FBI focuses its messages on terrorists and kidnapping scenarios while ignoring "far more numerous acts by government agents that affect everyday Americans." The responsibility for investigating police homicides can fall to journalists and civil society, whose efforts can also be protected by strong encryption.[4] Ball expressed his belief that mechanisms for exceptional access by government would increase the amount of government surveillance without making any of us any safer, and that the downsides of this increased surveillance would be experienced most acutely by vulnerable populations. He pointed to an argument articulated by Black Lives Matter activist Malkia Cyril that encryption is necessary for civil and human rights to prosper because it protects the democratic right to organize for change. According to Ball, Cyril also pointed to evidence that police surveillance has already been directed at nonviolent movements for police reform via scraping of social media accounts and seizure of smartphones from arrested activists. Ball said that evidence of the extrajudicial use of cell phone surveillance devices such as StingRay for metadata tracking suggests that this type of surveillance

---

[3] Daesh is the Arabic-language acronym for the terrorist group also known as the Islamic State, the Islamic State of Iraq and the Levant (ISIL), and the Islamic State of Iraq and Syria (ISIS).

[4] In the workshop, "strong encryption" was generally used to mean encryption schemes without exceptional access mechanisms. However, it was sometimes used to mean encryption believed to be strong based on current theory, known attack methods, and estimates of computing capacity available to an attacker. The latter definition, depending on one's views of the risks associated with exceptional access, might or might not include encryption schemes that provide exceptional access.

is a significant problem. Ball noted that the examples he highlighted were selected because they involve America and its allies. Encryption is also crucial to human rights work in countries like Syria, Russia, Iran, China, and Venezuela, but he said examples illustrating America's history of illegal surveillance of its own citizens and of alliances with perpetrators of war crimes and genocide should "give us pause" about giving the U.S. government exceptional access to encrypted data. Recognizing that the government has argued and will continue to argue that encrypted data without exceptional access impedes legitimate investigations against "heinous perpetrators," he urged the audience to focus on the big picture, arguing that exceptional access would help the FBI solve only a small number of cases compared with the great benefits of strong encryption for civil society globally. In addition, he posited that if given a "golden key," the FBI could use the key, or intelligence gathered using it, as a bargaining chip in discussions with other countries' law enforcement agencies, thus undermining the security of human rights workers abroad in order to support what he described as the FBI's short-term interests.

From his years at HRDAG, Ball has seen firsthand how encryption has saved the lives of people working to protect human rights. He expressed strong doubts that it would be wise to give any government an exceptional access key and argued that doing so would significantly degrade security for everyone. He suggested that the primary goal of cybersecurity should be, first and foremost, to protect people by providing tools that ensure strong electronic security against repressive governments, cybercriminals, and terrorists.

INTRODUCTORY REMARKS BY JAMES BAKER

James Baker, general counsel for the FBI, opened his remarks with an acknowledgement that the law enforcement community needs help from the various other communities represented at the workshop to ensure that America achieves its objectives while staying true to its values. In response to Ball's comments, he noted that his direct experience with the FBI, which has spanned 25 years, has given him a very different view from Ball's regarding the bureau's ethic and values. While openly recognizing that the FBI has made mistakes, both in the past and the present, he said the way Ball described the FBI shows "an organization with which I am not familiar . . . it's just not how we operate." The rest of Baker's talk focused on three main points: (1) strong encryption has benefits, (2) strong encryption has costs, and (3) the bureau does not seek to impose a specific solution but rather looks to the people to determine what tools are appropriate for it to use in carrying out its mission. Baker asserted that the FBI supports strong encryption and recognizes the tremendous benefits it offers, domestically and internationally, for cybersecurity, civil society, freedom of expression, and freedom of association. He also acknowledged that "the encryption genie is out of the bottle" and said that the FBI's challenge is to figure out how to function in the context of this new reality.

While agreeing with Ball's remarks about the value of encryption for protecting oppressed groups, Baker pointed out that the use of encryption also comes with costs. In particular, he focused on what the FBI views as costs to public safety, due to impediments facing the law enforcement, national security, and intelligence communities, stemming from the use of encryption. Under its mission to protect Americans and uphold the Constitution, the FBI must conduct investigations against foreign and domestic threats and enforce the criminal laws of the United States. In support of these activities, the bureau uses a variety of investigative tools, including interviews, human sources, subpoenas, and surveillance and searches, which involve physical places and people as well as data and electronic devices. As strong encryption grows more ubiquitous in the United States and around the world, the FBI's ability to access stored data and the content of real-time communications, also called "data in motion,"[5] for its investigations is affected. Although agents can and do try to work around these roadblocks by using other investigative methods, Baker said there are costs to this. For example, such alternative strategies may slow down investigations, lead to larger resource requirements, or yield less complete information than would otherwise have been obtained. Baker emphasized that the FBI is not trying to impose a particular solution, and he pointed out that the workshop would not have been convened if the bureau had had a solution. He explicitly noted that the FBI is not demanding a magic key for access, nor does it necessarily think that such a strategy would be the right solution.

---

[5] This term was used by workshop participants to refer to data in transit on a communications network and was used in contrast to "data at rest," or data that's stored on a mobile phone, laptop, server, or other computer device.

Baker said that the aim of the bureau is to communicate to the public the costs of encryption and to stimulate debate about the proper balance of equities, such as privacy, free expression, cybersecurity, innovation, competitiveness of American companies, and public safety. He suggested that it is not up to the FBI or companies to decide on the proper balance of equities; rather, it is up to the American people to decide this. He said that the FBI will use whatever tools the people make available to pursue its mission of protecting the American people and upholding the Constitution. He suggested that there are many questions that the country needs to answer. For example, What tools do we want law enforcement to have? How should we balance all of the different values at play? Are there technical solutions to make such a balance possible? He noted the possibility that such solutions may not be available, and we will have to accept the costs in one area or another.

Baker concluded with a reminder that the costs of encryption are not hypothetical: Real people will be affected by the ability of law enforcement to investigate and prevent a variety of criminal threats.

DISCUSSION

Panelists and other invited speakers engaged in an open discussion of the encryption landscape, moderated by Fred Cate.

Law Enforcement Capabilities and the Costs of Encryption

Cate opened the discussion by asking Baker to clarify his statements about the costs that encryption has for investigations. Baker first stated that in addition to the FBI and other federal agencies, there are 18,000 police forces in the United States. Each agency has different resources and different experiences with encryption. One impediment that commonly arises for state and local law enforcement is the inability to access data at rest on smartphones. When a phone is encrypted, with the contents accessible only by entering the passcode created by its owner, law enforcement has no technical tools to access the data it contains. Baker described this challenge as particularly acute for state and local authorities, adding that the FBI also faces it. Although he did not have specific numbers for the impact of this across the country, he said that the Manhattan District Attorney's office has 175 to 200 phones that fall into that category right now, which, after extrapolation, suggests that it is a significant issue affecting a large number of investigations across the country.

Baker also pointed to the ways the inability to track data in motion can also affect national security and intelligence activities. ISIL actors in Iraq and Syria, for example, typically initiate contact with U.S. residents online via social media channels that the FBI can track because they are unencrypted. As these relationships develop, however, ISIL actors instruct their contacts to switch over to communication channels that are strongly encrypted. Once that happens, the FBI can access only the metadata, not the actual content of messages. Baker said this situation is particularly problematic in today's terrorism climate, in which U.S. residents self-radicalize over a very short period of time. In the past, groups like Al Qaeda had a much more structured process for recruiting U.S.-based agents that involved face-to-face interaction and foreign travel, but today, U.S. residents are carrying out terrorist attacks after only online (and often encrypted) communications.

Later in the discussion, Marc Donner, engineering site director at Uber, asked how much technological capability the FBI has in this realm. James Burrell, deputy assistant director of the FBI, said that the bureau's overall budget for operational technology was on the order of several hundred million dollars. He noted that the FBI actually develops new technology specifically for its operations, rather than simply adapting existing technology, and that this capability must be developed to support operations in both national security and law enforcement contexts. With a finite budget and a limited number of highly trained personnel to support its multiple goals, Burrell said, the bureau must prioritize requirements across the spectrum of its responsibilities.

Richard Littlehale, assistant special agent in charge of the Tennessee Bureau of Investigation's (TBI's) Technical Services Unit, spoke from the perspective of state law enforcement, which he said faces a different set of problems from those faced by federal law enforcement. Although state and local law enforcement can request help from the FBI to some extent, it is often limited by its operational technology capacity and by the fact that many local law enforcement agencies have no operational technology division. Given the growing ubiquity of encryption, local agencies are encountering technological hurdles in case after case, and often it is not the perpetrator's phone but the victim's phone they seek to gain entry to. In such cases, he said, "were they to have a voice, perhaps they would want law enforcement to have access to their communications or their data." This means that encryption has a real, human cost, both internationally and domestically, but this is a cost TBI is still struggling to quantify. He suggested that some sort of relative harms analysis could help to elucidate these issues to support informed decision making about how to balance these costs.

Baker built on this point, noting that it is particularly hard to quantify the cost of encryption hurdles when this cost involves evidence that is not collected or a wiretap that is not pursued. At the FBI, if a device or communication is inaccessible, agents will not waste resources pursuing a warrant or wiretap, knowing that the data gained would be encrypted anyway. Unfortunately, it is hard to quantify the number of times this occurs, or what is lost in such situations.

Do We Have More Data, or Less?

Cate asked the panelists to comment on the argument that while today there are more data than ever that could potentially be available for government investigations, fewer and fewer data are accessible for those purposes. Baker agreed that there are more data and noted that the FBI uses every legal tool it has to obtain and analyze metadata, which can offer hints and illuminate networks of people who may be working together. However, he said metadata alone cannot give the FBI a full picture; often, the actual content is necessary to understand people's intent, capabilities, and plans. In addition, the deluge of metadata creates a data management problem, requiring agents to sort through a lot of noise to get to the pieces that can be informative.

Ball added his thoughts that governments have been able to use metadata to follow activists' communications. Indeed, from the viewpoint of social movements, metadata can be "as big a problem as content analysis, and one that's much more difficult . . . for them to protect themselves against." He said that Black Lives Matter is a movement in which activists are concerned that their lawful activities are being surveilled using metadata.

Asked to clarify how his remarks relate to encryption and not just surveillance in general, Ball stated that introducing layers of encryption could better protect social media-based communication from surveillance. Such capabilities have not yet been introduced, and he fears they may never be, either because doing so is technically difficult or because companies might be concerned that such a design would become compromised or illegal in the near future. Ball pointed to 2016 draft legislation by Senators Richard Burr and Dianne Feinstein,[6] which would have required technology companies to decrypt data at a court's request, as a worrisome harbinger of movement in this direction.

Which Tools Should We Entrust to the Government?

Inglis expressed his agreement with Baker's assessment of the FBI and its values and also agreed with Ball's arguments about the importance of encryption and other security tools for protecting individuals in the context of human rights. He then responded to the question of whether exceptional access is fundamentally different from other tools that the government has at its disposal. He noted that, even if exceptional access is not available, a variety of other tools are, and one could ask whether the government should be trusted with any of those. Many of the powers we entrust to the government—such as the power to tax, the power to indict, and the power to imprison—can be used for good and noble purposes, but also have the potential for misuse. He suggested that exceptional access was no different in this regard.

Later the discussion returned to this topic, and Ball urged the audience to question the assumption that government exceptional access is a good thing. Given his direct experience with governments that actively suppress their citizens' human rights, he believes that these are exactly the kind of governments that most want exceptional access; as examples, he pointed to North Korea and Cuba as governments that have made cryptography illegal, and to China

---

[6] Dianne Feinstein, U.S. Senator, "Intelligence Committee Leaders Release Discussion Draft of Encryption Bill," press release, April 13, 2016, http://www.feinstein.senate.gov/public/index.cfm/2016/4/intelligence-committee-leaders-release-discussion-draft-of-encryption-legislation.

and Russia as countries that have pursued government access to encrypted information. It is important to consider how many people can be helped by government exceptional access versus how many people can be harmed, a balance he believes skews strongly in the direction of greater harm under conditions of greater government access.

As for the FBI's ethic and activities, Ball expressed appreciation for Baker's clarification but countered that the FBI "looks very different from outside than it does from inside," particularly from the viewpoint of those involved in movements for social change. He suggested that surveillance, even of metadata, can have a chilling effect that is "in a palpable way harming our democracy."

Dealing with Encryption in an International Context

Inglis said that because encryption knows no national boundaries, a national solution would be insufficient and what is needed is a solution that works in an international context. Such a solution would be possible only when agreement on common foundational values can be reached, which he believes is possible even across international boundaries.

Kevin Bankston, director of the Open Technology Institute at the New America Foundation, tied this idea into Baker's remarks about encryption being widely used by entities like ISIS. According to research conducted by the New America Foundation,[7] out of the nine encrypted messaging apps ISIS recommends for its agents, eight are not U.S.-made, or are open source, or are both, which makes it hard for the U.S. government to control them. As this survey and the Schneier et al. survey[8] show, Bankston said, even if the U.S. government were able to gain exceptional access to systems created by U.S.-based companies, it would not fully solve the problem.

Inglis argued that it would not make sense for the United States to seek a solution that only works domestically, first because governments that share common value systems need to pursue common goals, and second, because companies—which exist in a global marketplace—need to have a common set of rules to adhere to across the jurisdictions in which they operate. Rather, in his view, we would be obligated to try to seek solutions in an international context, akin to the efforts undertaken in the context of nuclear proliferation, chemical weapons, and other arenas. Baker concurred that a solution has to work within a global context and affirmed Bankston's suggestion that the widespread global availability of encryption tools is one of the hardest problems to grapple with.

Bankston expressed his doubts that a global solution is realistic, arguing that an attempt to squelch end-to-end encryption globally would be "akin to trying to win the War on Drugs if drugs required no ingredients, could be endlessly and easily replicated, and could be smuggled over the Internet."

Inglis countered that in other ways the War on Drugs is not such a bad analogy, because drugs have both a benign and harmful purpose, and because although it is perhaps impossible to come up with a perfect solution, we still try. Rather than a stark choice between supporting either individual interests or collective national security, Inglis suggested that we should seek a solution that supports both aims in a way that is better, even if not perfect.

Noting that it is likely easier to regulate what happens on devices that are physically inside the United States, Baker said the potential business repercussions of such a move would also need to be considered, given that American companies must exist in a global marketplace.

Context Dependence of Government Needs and Obligations

Orin Kerr, the Fred C. Stevenson Research Professor of Law at the George Washington University Law School and workshop planning committee member, suggested that different solutions—and perhaps different levels of international coordination—might be warranted when dealing with encryption for national security purposes, as opposed to in the context of law enforcement, pointing out that there are three main contexts for government exceptional access: intelligence gathering for national security, federal criminal investigations, and state and local

---

[7] K. Bankston, R. Schulman, and J. Laperruque, 2015, "An Illustrative Inventory of Widely-Available Encryption Applications," New American Open Technology Institute, https://static.newamerica.org/attachments/12155-the-crypto-cat-is-out-of-the-bag/Crypto_Cat_Jan.0bea192f15424c9fa4859f78f1ad6b12.pdf.

[8] B. Schneier, K. Seidel, and S. Vijayakumar, 2016, "A Worldwide Survey of Encryption Products," Berkman Center Research Publication No. 2016-2, available at Social Science Research Network, http://ssrn.com/abstract=2731160.

criminal investigations. He asked whether members of Congress, when considering policy options, should think about different solutions or contexts for different purposes. Inglis observed that certain aspects of a potential international effort in this arena are likely to work much better in the context of law enforcement than in the context of national security or national intelligence, where countries inherently have different needs and goals.

Inglis went on to say that, at the national level, law enforcement and intelligence agencies have different standpoints on encryption, owing to their different missions, and citizens might feel more comfortable granting certain authorities to one than to another. The FBI and the NSA might, for instance, be placed under different obligations to disclose vulnerabilities they discover and use in investigations.

For example, he suggested that if the NSA uncovered a way to break into indigenous encrypted information channels from a rogue nation that is pursuing a nuclear weapon, few would expect the NSA to make that vulnerability known to such an adversary. But if the FBI uncovers a flaw in a system during an investigation, its obligations to both individual rights and collective security could well lead us to expect that the FBI would make such a vulnerability known so that it could be fixed.

Daniel Kahn Gillmor, senior staff technologist at the American Civil Liberties Union's Speech, Privacy, and Technology Project, suggested that there is essentially no widely or intensively used encryption system that could be considered indigenous to a particular organization, with few exceptions (one being Mujahedeen Secrets). If all players are using the same operating systems and software frameworks, flaws—whether in individual components or the overall system—would be common across all systems. As a result, if a government agency exploits a vulnerability when targeting an adversary, that would mean that those same systems would also be vulnerable for the people that the government is supposed to be supporting, he argued. Moreover, he added, by exploiting the vulnerability, the government may, in effect, hand over the exploit to the adversary.

Inglis contended that even if the mathematics underlying the system is the same, what matters is the instantiation of the mathematics-based protocol in the system, arguing that it is conceivable that a government agency could uncover a vulnerability unique to a certain organization, and in such a case, it might not be obligated to disclose the vulnerability.

Lessons from History

Butler Lampson, technical fellow at Microsoft and adjunct professor of computer science and electrical engineering at the Massachusetts Institute of Technology, suggested that studying the history of government and individual privacy could aid the debate about exceptional access in the context of encryption. For example, because of that history, today we have rules that guide when the government can enter a home or wiretap a phone.

Weighing in on this point, Inglis said that the Fourth Amendment (protection from unreasonable search and seizure) settled the matter, recognizing that there are times when the government is allowed to encroach on individual rights and expectations of privacy given probable cause. Today's challenge is how to deal with encryption in this context. FBI director James Comey, in Inglis's view, has no choice but to ask for the tools he needs to carry out the FBI's mission. The history of technology, Inglis said, is that it does not present any perfect solutions—only workable ones.

Baker concurred, stating his view that the Fourth Amendment gives law enforcement the authority to access information on, for example, an iPhone found at a crime scene or on procurement of a warrant when the data are inaccessible after demonstrating probable cause. The issue in the case of encryption is that, even with a warrant, the FBI today might not actually be able to access content that it is legally authorized to read, because the communication is encrypted. When the courts grant a warrant or wiretap, we can assume this is lawful behavior, and the government should be allowed past the encryption, Baker said. Building on this point, Lampson reasoned that the law does not protect the contents of his house from search under a government warrant and suggested that the contents of his phone are not fundamentally any different, a conclusion with which Inglis expressed agreement.

Ball drew from history a different perspective, pointing to instances where government powers have been abused. Rather than these events being viewed as anomalies, he said, it is reasonable to assume that similar abuses will continue to be perpetrated today and in the future.

Andrew Sherman, head of security practice at Eden Technologies, a New York City-based information technology consultancy, pointed to other lessons that might be drawn from the analog world. For example, he said, although the police may have the right to search a particular house, that does not mean they should have a master key to access all houses at any time. In the context of radio transmitters, those wary of eavesdropping might remove the batteries from their device—or place it inside a Faraday cage to block the signal—to avoid being tracked. In the case of protecting data that are stored or communicated, the solution people turn to is encryption, and although it might complicate things for investigators, it is not going away.

Susan Landau, professor of cybersecurity studies at Worcester Polytechnic Institute, suggested that today's technology raises new questions that are not addressed by wiretap laws developed in the past. For example, content and metadata today go well beyond the sender, receiver, and time of the call, and phones contain a great deal of information that a user might not even be aware of.

Practical Considerations

Eric Rescorla, a fellow in the office of the chief technology officer at Mozilla, pointed out that the term "possible" is being heavily used to talk about exceptional access and suggested that the more important question is really about what is "practical." Instead of debating whether something is theoretically possible, we should ask whether an exceptional access mechanism could actually be built and operated in a plausible way. To that end, he asked three broader technology questions to discover what might make a particular scheme or not. (1) How would such a mechanism actually interface with existing or new products to provide exceptional access, and how would that mechanism impact the security of those products? (2) Is it likely that such a mechanism could be evaded? (3) Is it practical to build an exceptional access mechanism that effectively allows access only to authorized users?

Joseph Lorenzo Hall, chief technologist at the Center for Democracy and Technology, cautioned that not every desired capability is, in fact, practical to build, because the technical strategy for achieving that capability may also harm the system in which it is being deployed. He suggested that a positive outcome of these discussions might be to enable communication about the limitations of our technical capabilities to nontechnical individuals.

Final Remarks from Panelists

Inglis framed the issue as one of differing goals. Individuals set their own agendas, but governments provide collective security. A key question, he asserted, is who aligns those aims. Practically speaking, if these decisions are left to market forces, companies will have many different answers and the implications are potentially akin to the disastrous results when nations largely leave their financial systems to market forces. Instead, he argued, society must choose the kind of security it wants. Later, Baker concurred with the suggestion that taking no action would essentially mean leaving the question to market forces.

Inglis cautioned against another potential "default" scenario, in which the private sector essentially says to the government "you're going to have to hack me." In his view, that would not be a particularly beneficial relationship for the government, the private sector, or the citizens. He suggested instead that if the government gains exceptional access to encrypted information, it should be done overtly and transparently, so that the public can understand how the access mechanisms work and the purposes for which they can be applied. Baker later expanded on this point, stating that while the FBI can hack into devices and can invest in further building up such capabilities, this process is slow, expensive, and fragile, because vulnerabilities that are identified are soon fixed. This approach also is not scalable to allow gaining information from many different devices, as is often necessary when dealing with a network of people.

Inglis expressed his belief that this debate is important enough to make it worth going beyond what seems practical and exploring the realm of what is possible. Looking to the architectures already in use by Google and cloud computing services that will essentially give a user exceptional access if they lose their key or that give a company exceptional access for business purposes, he posited that such systems might represent an approach that has proven secure enough (while providing some forms of exceptional access) that people are willing to buy into it in large numbers.

Ball then commented that quantifying the costs of having unbreakable encryption versus the costs of requiring lawful access is both a hard and interesting problem. He stated that the costs of a world in which all secrets are known by law enforcement will be counterfactuals—the movements that did not organize or the protests against unjust policies that did not mobilize. He said that these costs are difficult to quantify.

Ball noted that "everyone thinks they're the good guy," warning that believing one is working toward a good and higher purpose can at times lead people to choose means that are unsavory because they seem justified by the ends.

In his final remarks, Baker echoed the sentiment that it is worth reaching for the possible, likening the current state to a "pre-iPad" frame of mind in which we cannot imagine a different framework simply because we have not thought of it yet. Suggesting that there could be a solution that has not yet presented itself, he said that perhaps what we should seek is some way to "think different."

4

Session 2. Use Cases and the Feasibility of Segmenting Encryption Policies

The workshop's second session focused on the feasibility of segmenting encryption policies, for example, by creating avenues for government access to plaintext for certain types of information, certain types of users, or certain layers of information.

The session began with a brief exploration of use cases presented by Marc Donner. The discussion was moderated by planning committee members Fred Chang, director of the Darwin Deason Institute for Cyber Security at Southern Methodist University, and Susan Landau.

Drawing from his past experience working in the finance industry and with Google Health, Donner used the finance and health care sectors to illustrate how industries handle highly sensitive information, including their use of encryption.

In the context of finance, Donner described the complex networks of data holders, data flows, and transit points involved in carrying out daily transactions in both consumer banking and institutional finance. While some links are encrypted and there are set processes for protecting data, he said these practices are not consistently employed. Data in transit from one node to another is typically encrypted, but most core databases are not encrypted, largely due to the sheer number of people who must access these databases on a constant basis. He noted that a system like Google Keystore, which provides an encryption key for each data item, is a potentially viable approach in this context and could be implemented if legacy systems can be fixed to accommodate this.

In the context of health care, Donner said that as in the financial industry, most systems do not use encryption for data in storage. Where encryption is incorporated, it is done largely for data in transit or for stored information at the level of individual departments or laboratories rather than systemwide. A further complication, he said, is that health care providers are struggling with tough questions surrounding what information to share with consumers—and how best to share it—when most systems are organized to share information among care providers and insurers and thus not structured or communicated in ways that would be appropriate for consumers. In addition, he cited Google's abandoned effort to accumulate consumers' medical data (an effort called Google Health, which he ran for 2.5 years and shut down) to illustrate the argument that consumers are afraid of concentrating their medical data, which he attributed partly to weaknesses in the health system and partly to weaknesses embedded in policy structure.

Broadly speaking, Donner speculated that the reason encryption is not more widely used in these industries is because decision makers do not perceive a need for it. This is further complicated by the fact that many are focused on the more basic struggle of staying ahead of the information-sharing needs that are central to their daily business. He said institutions are "chewing away at the problem," but incorporating encryption more broadly requires a change in the organization of systems, and doing so without interrupting the delivery of daily services is challenging. Returning to the idea of implementing a system such as Google Keystore, Donner said if data at rest are encrypted, then people with system privileges will have to retrieve a key to access the data, which, in a well-managed system, will leave footprints that can be tracked. While recognizing that implementing such a key management system is not free or easy, he said it is possible.

Regarding the different treatment of data in transit as compared to data at rest, Donner noted that there might not be much of a difference between the two from a communications theory standpoint, but one important difference is that an encryption key for data in transit can be discarded after the end of the communication, whereas with stored data, the encryption key needs to be preserved and managed until the data can be discarded.

DISCUSSION

Institutional Context

In a broader discussion, participants considered how various aspects of an institution's context influence the need, desirability, and technical framework for exceptional access.

Broadly speaking, when considering whether exceptional access is possible or desirable, it is useful to consider demonstrated attitudes toward information sharing in various sectors. On the whole, Donner said, the healthcare and finance industries want to comply with government requests and are eager to respond when asked for information. Andrew Sherman reiterated this point with regard to these industries, saying government wouldn't need exceptional access to his laptop because the source data for it came from a system to which "the legal department would gladly give you access with the right paperwork." In addition, Donner likened most institutional databases to a "maze of twisty passages," suggesting that anyone seeking access, exceptional or otherwise, to most corporate data would likely need someone from the institution to help navigate the database to find the desired information anyway. Given this context, he posited that it likely is not reasonable to expect the government to expend the resources necessary to use a backdoor to tap into such databases when the institution could simply be directly asked to provide the information.

Speaking to the role that device encryption plays in protecting corporate data, Guy L. "Bud" Tribble, vice president of software technology at Apple, raised the point that although many corporate databases may have been sitting on a relatively secure server when they were initially set up, some part of the data may end up on a laptop or mobile device. Donner replied that this happens frequently and suggested that the consequences of such events largely depend on how well run the institution is. A larger, well-run institution (which he defined as one that has an established information technology department) would require full-disk encryption on laptops or mobile devices; however, there are many smaller institutions that do not have such a requirement. Kevin Bankston reiterated the point that when data on corporate mobile devices and laptops is encrypted, it is being protected by the same full-disk encryption as all other consumer products, and thus any vulnerabilities that may be created by mandated mechanisms for exceptional access would extend to a variety of sectors, including health and finance. Therefore, Bankston continued, it is not possible to segment encryption policy as between consumer and corporate data, because consumer software and devices are also widely used in a variety of corporate sectors.

Vertical Segmentation

Participants moved into a discussion about the feasibility of strategies for allowing government access to plaintext in a way that is segmented either vertically (i.e., by sector or user) or horizontally (i.e., segmented according to different technological layers, such as a phone's operating system versus in applications that run on that operating system).

Eric Rescorla questioned whether it is possible to "wall off" the use of strong encryption in specific sectors when the security of these systems depends on the same commodity products used by all other applications. For example, he said, when you interact with your stockbroker, you are likely using the same browser that you use to interact with Facebook and the same voice-over IP system that you use to talk with your doctor. As such, he questioned whether it was possible to allow "stronger" encryption—in this case, meaning encryption without exceptional access—to some applications but not others.

It is largely impractical for institutions to build their own encryption tools, Donner said, and as a result, when encryption is used in various sectors, it is based on standard, commercially available products. The difference, in his experience, is how well institutions manage their security activities. Getting consensus around what to encrypt and how to encrypt it is a significant challenge, because sectors like finance and health care are rapidly changing, they involve complex, interacting work flows rather than simple transactions, and require supple yet powerful access control mechanisms.

Butler Lampson suggested that from a practical standpoint, the feasibility of walling off exceptional access for certain sectors would depend on the ability to escrow the encryption keys for one application separately from the keys for other applications such that one could access different sets of keys for different purposes.

Brian LaMacchia, director of the Security and Cryptography Group at Microsoft Research, pointed to lessons learned in the 1990s about the pitfalls of effectively deploying "stronger" and "weaker" security for different contexts. At that time, companies would build worldwide products with "weak encryption" (meaning small key size, easily crackable by a reasonably resourced attacker) built in and then offer a "high encryption pack," which added "strong encryption" capabilities to the product, to U.S. and Canadian customers only. Microsoft shipped "high encryption packs" for operating systems through Windows 2000. In 2000, U.S. export controls changed such that operating systems including strong encryption could generally be shipped worldwide, and the need for splitting out a high-encryption pack went away.

During the period when export controls were in effect, Microsoft added a "server-gated cryptography" feature to its Web browser Internet Explorer to allow selection of strong cryptography when connecting to servers outfitted with special certificates for their server keys, even if the underlying Windows operating system only supported weak encryption, LaMacchia said. Netscape implemented a similar feature for its browser that it called "International Step-Up." The result, according to LaMacchia, was a mix of confusion and unintended consequences; while Microsoft forged a workable solution, it was difficult to test and deploy and also difficult to remove once export controls changed a few years later and server-gated cryptography was no longer needed. This export-control architecture is still deployed and continues to be a source of vulnerabilities, he added.

Lampson raised the concern that the fundamental goals of what would be accomplished by vertically segmented exceptional access have not been adequately articulated, making it impossible to envision a technical solution to achieve such a goal. Given that, for example, medical data involve many different kinds of data that are held by different parties and for different purposes, it is extremely difficult to imagine how one could possibly provide stronger cryptography for medical data.

Horizontal Segmentation

Given a general sense that segregating where exceptional access would or would not be required by sector is difficult, Landau moved the conversation toward the feasibility of segregating exceptional access horizontally. What, for example, would be the implications of requiring exceptional access at the platform layer but not at the application layer?

Daniel Kahn Gillmor said that in his view, there would be no way to make sense of such segregation from an engineering perspective, because if we require exceptional access at the operating system layer, someone will just make an operating system that doesn't provide the exceptional access. Landau countered with the argument that an operating system is not easily made and widely deployed in the same way that apps are. Gillmor further observed that, if you were to require exceptional access at the hardware level (i.e., providing access to the plaintext of what is stored in random access memory), then ultimately you have provided access to all of the data, so segmentation is impossible when the lowest layers are vulnerable.

Tribble agreed that it is hard to imagine a way to effectively segment exceptional access horizontally. He added that it is probably feasible for apps to evade built-in exceptional access mechanisms, for example, by using a key that is in the user's head and not stored on the device.

Building on these ideas, Rescorla cited the Communications Assistance for Law Enforcement Act as an example where law enforcement was provided access to the bottom layer of the communications stack by requiring carriers to provide access to the raw data. However, applications can encrypt the data, and carriers have no obligation to provide data they don't have. Any requirement that ensures access at lower layers necessarily is very difficult and involves breaking boundaries between different pieces of the system.

LaMacchia expanded on this point, explaining that segmenting horizontally would require engineers to break "abstraction boundaries" that are crucial to the integrity of computer programs. Abstraction boundaries are rigid design boundaries built into programs that serve to break a "hard problem"—that is, the overall function of the program as a whole—into many simpler problems that, when linked together, achieve the desired goal. This approach enhances security because each component can be built securely and engineers know that the communication points between the components are a key place to focus when defending against malicious behavior by another component. Breaking the abstraction boundaries, as a result, adds complexity, makes vulnerabilities more likely, makes it harder to maintain the software, and makes it more difficult to track and fix problems.

Wrapping up, Lampson said the problem of horizontal segmentation is compounded by the fact that apps operate essentially independently of operating systems, so building an exceptional access system that prevents apps from using superencryption[1] would be exceedingly difficult.

---

[1] Superencryption involves first encrypting using an encryption algorithm of the user's choosing and then encrypting a second time using a preferred or mandated encryption algorithm, such as one that enables exceptional access.

5

Session 3. Security Risks of Architectures for Enabling Government Access to Plaintext

In the workshop's third session, participants drilled deeper into the technical options for creating exceptional access mechanisms, discussed how these options might impact cybersecurity, and explored the motivations of and constraints on the government, industry, and society more broadly.

The session began with a presentation by Matt Blaze, associate professor of computer and information science at the University of Pennsylvania. He explored the historical evolution of technological solutions for exceptional access and presented an overview of the challenges faced today. The presentation was followed by a wide-ranging discussion moderated by Fred Chang and Susan Landau.

HISTORICAL CONTEXT

Blaze began his presentation with a look at the history of cryptography and exceptional access, starting with wiretapping. Originally, wiretaps involved law enforcement getting access to the target's phone line and connecting a device capable of capturing the analog audio and telephone network signaling being sent over the line—a relatively straightforward proposition. Eventually, as telephone systems became digital, the Communications Assistance for Law Enforcement Act was enacted to ensure that carriers would provide law enforcement with the necessary interface to their networks as well.

Crypto War I

Blaze called the period from 1992 to 2000 "Crypto War I," the time during which consumers, the government, and the telecommunications industry grappled with dramatic shifts in the encryption landscape. Blaze pegs the start of this "war" to AT&T's 1992 release of the TSD-3600, a secure telephone for consumers akin to the secure phones that had previously been used only by the government. The TSD-3600s used a Diffie-Hellman key exchange to set up encryption keys and a 56-bit data encryption standard to encrypt the digitized audio.

Although the telephone was expensive and not widely sold, the U.S. government nonetheless feared that technology like the TSD-3600 would spell the end of wiretapping and requested that AT&T make changes to accommodate lawful wiretaps on individuals who might use the device. The solution proposed was the Clipper Chip, which was designed by the National Security Agency (NSA) to be a drop-in replacement for the TSD-3600's data encryption chip. Using an enhanced algorithm called SkipJack, the Clipper Chip provided 80 bits of security as opposed to 56 bits. It also introduced key escrow, a feature that allowed the government to recover plaintext from a call if a TSD-3600 was used by a person who was the subject of an approved wiretap. AT&T incorporated the Clipper Chip into all TSD-3600 phones and even recalled already-sold TSD-3600 phones that lacked the chip, Blaze recounted.

The Clipper Chip was a controversial proposal and had technical problems, Blaze said. The first problem was that protocol failures in the chip's design made it easy to bypass the key escrow feature; Blaze discovered some of these failures himself while working for AT&T. Although bypassability was likely a fundamental problem with the design, the protocol failures found by Blaze were comparatively minor and could be patched. Ultimately, a series of larger problems led to the Clipper Chip's demise by the dawn of the 21st century. One key problem, in Blaze's view, was that the Clipper Chip turned an inherently inexpensive technology for software-implemented cryptography into a hardware-based model that was expensive and difficult to integrate into the system. The Clipper Chip was built on a particular structure for performing encryption and required specific, tamper-resistant hardware and a classified algorithm that could not be made public. In addition, said Blaze, it had a central key database, which, although split between two government agencies, ultimately "amplified the risks extraordinarily by basically creating an end-to-end encryption system that was not, in fact, end-to-end." This ultimately led to a system that was expensive, riskier, and easily bypassed.

By 2000, Blaze said, the country had come to the conclusion that the use of encryption was "really too important to slow down" by requiring a key escrow system for government access, and "unfettered cryptography" was allowed to blossom.

Blaze noted that an unfortunate side effect of the focus on the Clipper Chip and key escrow systems during the 1990s was that insufficient attention was paid to the security standards being built into the communications and information infrastructure then in use, which many view as not having been sufficiently robust to support the sensitive applications that depended on it, such as commerce, finance, and national security. "We are paying that price to this day," Blaze said.

Crypto War II and the Cybersecurity Crisis

Blaze then turned to the current period, which he described as a time of both "Crypto War II" and a "cybersecurity crisis." The first term stems from the renewed debate over encryption spurred by comments from law enforcement and national security officials about the challenges posed by ubiquitous encryption, exemplified by an October 16, 2014, statement from Federal Bureau of Investigation (FBI) director James Comey:

> Unfortunately, the law hasn't kept pace with technology, and this disconnect has created a significant public safety problem. We call it "Going Dark," and what it means is this: Those charged with protecting our people aren't always able to access the evidence we need to prosecute crime and prevent terrorism even with lawful authority. We have the legal authority to intercept and access communications and information pursuant to court order, but we often lack the technological ability to do so.[1]

At the same time, a daily barrage of data breaches and other cybersecurity incidents is affecting our critical systems, said Blaze, offering as an example the enormous 2015 breach at the U.S. Office of Personnel Management. The United States depends on the same platforms produced for the broad consumer market—operating systems and smartphones, and the like—for its critical infrastructure, financial systems, economy, and national security, as it does for its personal or even frivolous activities. Blaze stated that the adversaries perpetrating these breaches are not only ordinary criminals but also nation-states, and that the problem of securing all of this critical infrastructure is getting steadily worse rather than better.

---

[1] From remarks of FBI director James Comey at the Brookings Institution on October 16, 2014, "Going Dark: Are Technology, Privacy, and Public Safety on a Collision Course?," https://www.fbi.gov/news/speeches/going-dark-are-technology-privacy-and-public-safety-on-a-collision-course.

Fundamentals of the Current Cybersecurity Landscape

Noting that the challenge of building reliable systems at scale has plagued computer science since the field's inception, Blaze said that, in general, we still "don't know how to fix this." However, he pointed to two approaches as providing partial solutions: reducing the number of components in a system and using cryptography. One tried-and-true approach, he said, is to make systems as small and simple as possible in order to reduce the footprint of the vulnerabilities. Despite the merits of this approach, it has not proven practical in a world in which the endless thirst for capabilities leads to systems that are ever larger and more complex. New features are added to systems too quickly to allow them to be properly understood and to be made more robust.

The second approach is cryptography. By encrypting the data used in large swaths of a system's components, we can reduce the "attack surface" and confine vulnerabilities to a smaller number of components. End-to-end encryption is considered the best practice in this area because it allows only the sender and receiver access to plaintext in the case of communication and allows only the person storing the data access in the case of data storage, thus reducing the opportunities for compromise to a bare minimum.

Looking forward, Blaze identified two crucial problems that need to be addressed and balanced. The first is that the U.S. computing infrastructure is in "terrible shape" and "getting worse," and that any actions taken should at a minimum do no harm. The second is that encryption and similar technologies are, may be, or will be making lawful access to communications more difficult. The challenge, he said, is to address both issues without worsening the first.

Exceptional Access: Considerations and Challenges

Blaze then turned to the concept of exceptional access, which he defined as a mechanism that provides access to plaintext that is not inherent to the requirements of the application itself. In his view, exceptional access, by nature, makes a system more complex and makes it impossible to provide end-to-end encryption because it essentially introduces an additional end point.

He pointed to two critical considerations relevant to the policy and technical feasibility of an exceptional access system. The first, "Can we trust the system *if* it works properly?" is a policy question. The second, "Can we trust the system *to* work properly?" is a technical question and is the focus of the current workshop.

Citing the report of which he is a coauthor, *Keys Under Doormats: Mandating Insecurity by Requiring Government Access to All Data and Communications*,[2] Blaze articulated some of the ways exceptional access is at odds with the need to better protect infrastructure. He said exceptional access necessarily makes cryptography weaker, increases the difficulty of integrating cryptography securely into applications and systems, creates operational vulnerabilities, and, in many cases, can be easily bypassed. Blaze pointed out that encryption systems can fail even if there are no additional complications from exceptional access. The most common reasons for such failures, Blaze said, have to do with the deployment of an encryption tool for a specific application—it is likely, say, that the tool does not meet some security requirement in the application, owing to some usability issue, or there may be problems with the application itself or the platform on which it is running. Problems with the engineering of the encryption tool, including implementation of the encryption algorithms, are also fairly common, he said. Less common, although still possible, are failures in the encryption algorithms or protocols themselves.

Although the algorithms and protocols are perhaps the easiest aspect of creating an encryption system that works, there are still weaknesses. Despite a great deal of mathematical work in this field, there is still no general theory of cryptography, Blaze posited. He called this "one of the dirty secrets of cryptography." Furthermore, occasionally it turns out that the assumptions underlying algorithms aren't entirely correct, he said. Protocols also can turn out to have weaknesses. As an example, he pointed to the protocol failures in the Clipper Chip, an encryption system designed by perhaps the world's best cryptographers at the time.

The biggest challenges to implementing exceptional access, Blaze said, would likely be related to design and software engineering, which are complicated by access requirements. As a result, he surmised, a requirement for

---

[2] H. Abelson R. Anderson, S.M. Bellovin, J. Benaloh, M. Blaze, W. Diffie, J. Gilmore, et al., 2015, *Keys Under Doormats: Mandating Insecurity by Requiring Government Access to All Data and Communications,* Technical Report MIT-CSAIL-TR-2015-026, Massachusetts Institute of Technology Computer Science and Artificial Intelligence Laboratory, July 6.

exceptional access may lead many vendors to reduce their focus on security or forego encryption altogether due to the increased difficulty and expense of building secure encryption systems that also allow for exceptional access. As a result, he said, there's a danger that "we won't see the deployment of encryption in places where we really, really need to have it used."

Exceptional access also raises several operational challenges. Whether keys are kept in a single centralized escrow system or in multiple systems, the result is collections of secrets "that have to be guarded essentially in perpetuity," Blaze noted. Moreover, the complexity of operational infrastructure needed to add exceptional access may well dwarf all the other operational requirements of the application. These collections of secrets would have enormous value for adversaries, creating high-value targets. Maintaining and securing such systems, he said, would be both extremely difficult and extremely expensive.

Allowing that exceptional access can be built into certain applications under certain circumstances at an acceptable cost (and indeed this has already been done in some cases), Blaze said that the risks of implementing exceptional access in a more generalized sense are enormous and the consequences going forward would be "unbounded and unpredictable." Moreover, Blaze observed, in the context of a fast-moving technology industry involving numerous smaller actors, it is likely exceedingly difficult to implement exceptional access generally, particularly in the nonenterprise context. And given an evolving cast of adversaries that increasingly includes nation-states seeking to do serious harm to the security and economy of the United States, any failures in this realm are likely to be both high impact and expensive.

DISCUSSION

Fred Chang and Susan Landau moderated a broader discussion of the technical options and security risks related to exceptional access to encrypted information and communications. The discussion is broken into two sections: The first focuses on context and major issues and the second on potential solutions. The order in which the contributions are presented here is not the order in which they were discussed at the workshop.

Part 1: Issues and Context

Security Trade-offs

Chang inquired as to whether, instead of pitting cybersecurity and exceptional access against each other as opposing choices, it would be reasonable to frame the issue as a series of engineering trade-offs. Blaze agreed with that conceptualization in principle but noted that as the technological landscape grows more complex and the stakes become higher, it becomes increasingly challenging to truly understand what is being traded or sacrificed. A related weakness, he added, is that we have poor metrics for evaluating the security of our systems.

Blaze described the difficulty of creating a secure exceptional-access system as "unprecedented." He noted that, although the problems are subtle and there is no specific proposed system on the table to evaluate, it is hard to quantify exactly what the risks are. At a fundamental level, such a system would likely require (1) a secret held somewhere, (2) a mechanism for communicating that secret, and (3) a mechanism for guarding that secret effectively in perpetuity. Compounding the complexity of these basic requirements is the fact that apps and software can be used anywhere—and by anyone—around the globe.

Noting improvements in cryptography and key management systems, Chang asked whether any recent technological breakthroughs might make exceptional access more feasible. Although he acknowledged incremental progress in cryptography and its algorithms, Blaze said that because the range of vulnerabilities, or "problem space," has also expanded, the ultimate result is a mixed bag in terms of how much progress has been made relative to the actual problems.

Daniel Kahn Gillmor spoke of the trade-off between the (perhaps limited) benefits of an exceptional access system to law enforcement and the increased vulnerability to which such a system would expose everyone. Although exceptional access might enhance law enforcement's ability to catch the "dumb criminals" (those without the resources or knowledge necessary to procure end-to-end encryption tools), he predicted that many others would rapidly adopt a less vulnerable encryption system, even if it were not available by default. Later, Patrick Ball reiterated this point, suggesting that sophisticated users will be able to circumvent exceptional access through what would amount to a form of steganography, by hiding secure encryption inside a layer of encryption with exceptional access. Until the outer layer is decrypted, an adversary or government would not even know that the material inside had been encrypted. Such a scheme, Ball said, would not be difficult for savvy users to implement; as a result, the only targets whose communications can be made visible through exceptional access schemes are "dumb criminals" and law-abiding citizens.

Gillmor emphasized that the costs of deploying exceptional access are borne by everyone. Even worse, in his view, we would be stuck with any downsides for years to come. A weakness in security was exploited in an analogous deployment in the 1990s to comply with U.S. regulations on the export of cryptography technologies. We are still paying the cost, Gillmor said, "even though we decided years ago that that was not a good cost to pay," for the introduction of export-grade cipher suites used by the Transport Layer Security and Secure Sockets Layer family of protocols.

Blaze noted some additional trade-offs. If, for example, a system is built with a centralized repository that application developers would make use of, this concentrates one part of the risk in a "fairly well hardened environment," but at the same time creates a "big central fat target" that may or may not be adequately secured. If the central repository fails, it fails catastrophically. Given the complexity of the requirements associated with exceptional access, he said it is quite likely that engineers designing one aspect of a system to meet one requirement could create a structural weakness somewhere else, perhaps without knowing it. Blaze went on to caution that the right set of requirements needs to be considered: It may be easy to meet the requirement that keys can be recovered, but that does not ensure that only the right people are recovering keys.

Landau raised two other trade-offs. First, if a smartphone's data are more easily accessible, it undermines the ability of the phone to act as a secure authenticator. The fact that everyone carries their phone with them—and we all notice when it's gone—makes it especially useful, she said, and losing this capability would impose a cost. Second, since the mid-1990s, the U.S. Department of Defense (DOD) has been using more and more off-the-shelf, commercial equipment, in part because of the speed of innovation in Silicon Valley. As a result, she observed, it is important to remember that DOD has a strong interest not just in the ability to break into encrypted devices or communication streams, but also in the ability to keep them secure.

Kevin Bankston explored how exceptional access mechanisms could create vulnerabilities that might be exploited. Bud Tribble agreed that operationalizing exceptional access at scale would indeed raise the risk that adversaries could tap into the decryption capability, pointing to that concern as one of the reasons Apple decided to implement end-to-end encryption. A requirement to maintain an exceptional access mechanism, he said, would create a persistent target for an adversary to exploit, a fundamentally riskier situation than the current system in which Apple can catch and patch security vulnerabilities as they become known.

Another issue to consider is how exceptional access would play out internationally—say, if a foreign government wanted to tap into a communications stream encrypted in a way that enables FBI access to the plaintext. Ball said that based on his experience working with human rights groups at risk of government persecution, faced with such a request, he "would be delighted to say 'I don't have the keys.'"

Finally, in a broader sense, there are trade-offs involved in action versus inaction relating to the alternative outcomes that might occur under different circumstances. Butler Lampson suggested that, in the absence of a credible technical solution from the technology community, legislators might come up with their own solution. At several points throughout the workshop, other participants pondered what might be sacrificed if the quest for a "perfect" solution is allowed to block the pursuit of workable, albeit imperfect, solutions.

The Law Enforcement Context

Participants discussed key concerns and challenges facing law enforcement related to data encryption.

Noting that companies will generally produce data that they have access to in response to law enforcement legal demands, Richard Littlehale asked why some companies are considered to provide adequate security even if they retain the ability to access encrypted data, while others argue that a total lack of access by anyone but the individual user is the only way to ensure adequate security.

At several points, Littlehale suggested that law enforcement is not seeking a perfect system of total access, but is instead looking to improve the current situation, where the increasing ubiquity of encryption for devices and communications is rapidly constraining the types of evidence accessible to law enforcement. In response to the point that technologically sophisticated criminals will likely continue to find ways to protect their data from law enforcement, Littlehale urged attendees not to underestimate the amount of human misery caused by criminals who are either "dumb" or "smart but lazy."

Littlehale underscored the fact that these issues are currently affecting real cases. If it is determined that exceptional access is either not technically feasible or not a policy the country wishes to pursue, what then is law enforcement expected to do to fulfill its mission? Blaze built on this point, noting that law enforcement and the FBI need viable alternatives if exceptional access does not work out. He predicted that a "Plan B" would involve more investment in lawful hacking and other forensics capabilities. This idea is discussed in greater depth below (see the section "Part 2: Exploring Solutions").

Joseph Lorenzo Hall suggested it will be important to measure the needs of law enforcement. Such insights would give society a more rational way to understand what is lost if more security is pursued at the expense of catching fewer perpetrators, or if we sacrifice security to achieve law enforcement goals. Landau commented that participants in the annual Workshop on the Economics of Information Security are pursuing research in this vein, but that it is often difficult to obtain the data needed to truly answer the question.

Littlehale agreed that these impacts are difficult to quantify. Rarely can law enforcement point to encrypted data as an absolute or insurmountable block to an investigation, he said; the typical impacts are more nuanced: cases take longer to investigate, and victims endure extra suffering as a result or resources are pulled from other cases. On the flip side, he said, it is appropriate to recognize the value of feeling secure, the feeling that one's privacy is protected.

Littlehale noted also that certain types of evidence previously available to law enforcement in the analog world are no longer available in the digital world. For example, under a physical search warrant, a police officer might once have patted down a suspect and found an address book. Now, a suspect's address book is likely to be stored on a smartphone, and its content is more and more often encrypted. In essence, he said, this means law enforcement is being expected to execute its mission—which includes not only prosecuting the guilty but exonerating the innocent—with potentially less evidence.

Ball offered a counterargument: today's digital world offers a great deal more information to law enforcement than was previously available, through means such as location tracking, metadata, unencrypted e-mails, and plaintext calls made through traditional cellular networks. Although we may be "going dark" in some places, we are going "brilliantly bright" in others, he argued, suggesting that abandoning our devices altogether would take a lot more evidence out of the reach of law enforcement than using fully encrypted devices would.

Addressing in a broader sense the aims of law enforcement, Littlehale noted that concerns about the potential for someone to steal an escrow key or abuse exceptional access to the detriment of human rights are also concerns of the law enforcement community. Such actions, he noted, would be crimes, and thus law enforcement has an interest in preventing and prosecuting them.

The Industry Context

Participants considered the market environment that has driven certain decisions by industry players, as well as how companies might respond to an exceptional access requirement.

From a practical standpoint, Blaze suggested that imposing an exceptional access system that is too complex or difficult to implement might drive many companies (with the possible exception of Apple, he conceded) to simply abandon encryption. Such an outcome would result in much less security for everyone.

Tribble explained that Apple's approach to implementing encryption has been a response to two trends: (1) an increasing level of threat to its customers and (2) the fact that consumers are keeping an increasing amount of important information on their phones. Given these trends, Apple opted to pursue end-to-end encryption, an approach, Tribble noted, that the technical community over the past 50 years has determined to be the best practice.

Tribble went on to acknowledge that when Apple does not have the keys to unlock something law enforcement needs access to, that can lead to a legal order not being enforceable, which, he conceded, is not a good thing. However, in the same way that it is hard to measure precisely how this impacts the efforts of law enforcement, it is hard to quantify the risks and benefits to customers whose data are protected (or not) with end-to-end encryption.

Noting that Apple recently introduced a feature that allows people to download their medical record to their phones, Tribble emphasized that these trends—rising threats and an increased amount of sensitive information on phones—are going to steepen in the coming years. Echoing a sentiment expressed earlier in the workshop by Baker, Tribble said the solutions to these problems are not for one company or one government agency to decide, but for society as a whole.

The Internet of Things

Landau moved the conversation toward the Internet of Things (IoT) to explore how the proliferation of network-connected devices affects the encryption landscape or exceptional access options. Although the IoT may seem trivial—for example, it may be unlikely that a network-connected toaster would reveal vital information—she pointed to the U.S. intelligence community's 2016 worldwide threat assessment that suggested "future intelligence services might use the IoT for identification, surveillance, monitoring, location tracking, and targeting for recruitment, or to gain access to network or user credentials."[3]

Eric Rescorla and Hall began by clarifying that many such devices do not or cannot practically use encryption. Hall remarked that some IoT devices take 10 seconds or more to perform an encryption, and those that do likely use the same TLS protocol that is widely used for Internet communications today. However, there are efforts to come up with lightweight cryptographic capabilities for such devices, said Hall. Andrew Sherman noted that many IoT devices involve constant watching or listening in private environments, which, depending on your viewpoint, could represent a tremendous opportunity or a tremendous risk.

James Burrell pointed to two main areas of concern from the law enforcement perspective: cybersecurity and forensics. Because the IoT introduces new devices into networks, a cyberattacker has many new points to attack. The compromise of a network-connected coffeemaker, for example, might not be useful on its own, but could be very valuable for an adversary if it allows access to other pieces of the network, he said. Burrell said that in the context of forensics, law enforcement would generally gain the most from being able to access data or communications from IoT devices at the point of data aggregation, where all of these devices are transmitting data to a cloud service or to a local hub, because direct physical access would otherwise be required. Later, Landau and Brian LaMacchia noted that in the absence of practical homomorphic encryption, data at the point of aggregation would need to be available as plaintext.

Littlehale offered a slightly different take, suggesting that physical devices themselves can prove useful to law enforcement. For example, in a homicide investigation, data stored from a sensing device could be accessed to discern when a person was or was not present in the home at a particular time. This type of information, he said, is already being used by law enforcement, although current uses typically involve devices that have a memory but no network connection.

Rescorla observed that the other speakers seemed to be saying that government would not need exceptional access to communications among IoT devices, because it would be able to extract needed data from the aggregation points. Littlehale responded that in the current environment, such access is likely not necessary, but it is unclear what the future may hold.

From a technical perspective, LaMacchia noted that for some portion of these devices—particularly ones meant to be built into houses, such as light switches—a major concern is the limited capability for security updates. Many low-end devices, he said, are based on a "rip and replace" model for updating, requiring new hardware for updates and not just new software. As a result, such devices are unlikely to be using up-to-date security. The ultimate result of this, he suggested, is likely to be a solution in which the more vulnerable pieces of a network are

---

[3] J.R. Clapper, "Worldwide Threat Assessment of the US Intelligence Community," Statement for the Record, Senate Select Committee on Intelligence, February 9, 2016, p. 1, http://www.intelligence.senate.gov/sites/default/files/wwt2016.pdf.

walled off with a series of internal firewalls so they do not compromise the more secure portions of the network. If exceptional access is something society decides it wants, LaMacchia said, it may not actually be possible to add that capability to devices that cannot be updated.

Building on this point, Donner pointed to modern cars as an example of a relatively mature instance of the IoT that has already revealed how weak security, mismanagement at the configuration level, and a lack of updatability can lead to significant problems. He suggested that the same essential problems are likely to happen "on a larger scale and on a faster time line" as the IoT expands. Stephen Checkoway of the University of Illinois, Chicago, noted that he was one of the people who had hacked into cars in 2010 to demonstrate some of these issues. He said that although the security story then was "kind of a disaster," things have improved somewhat, and manufacturers are developing the capability for over-the-air security updates.

Rescorla noted that because IoT devices often are actuators capable of causing things to happen in the physical world, it is especially important that any exceptional access mechanism not pose a threat to authentication and integrity. For instance, an attacker who gained write access to the control channel for such a device might be able to cause physical harm, such as a fire.

Prompted by a question from Chang about system-to-system traffic, Blaze noted that as the IoT expands, in general, these devices will reuse building blocks from other computing systems. Already, that has meant that entire operating systems once intended for a desktop computer are being incorporated into embedded devices, a trend Blaze expects to continue.

Noting that it is impossible to accurately predict how the IoT will evolve in the coming years, Blaze cautioned that the decisions made today about security infrastructure are going to have profound effects on the security of future platforms. Because decisions made now with respect to smartphones, for example, are likely to apply to a great diversity of IoT devices down the road, Blaze said that what we are doing today is immensely important.

Part 2: Exploring Solutions

Looking forward, participants brainstormed the types of requirements that might be considered when designing an exceptional access system. They also explored the feasibility and security implications of several specific technological and operational options.

Requirements for an Exceptional Access System

Several participants expressed frustration over a lack of clarity on what exactly an exceptional access system would need to do to meet the government's expressed needs. Chang challenged attendees to brainstorm a set of possible requirements.

Matt Green, assistant professor in the Department of Computer Science at Johns Hopkins University, proposed a key first set of questions around what form a mandate for access might take:

1. Would the government mandate exceptional access or only encourage companies to adopt it?
2. Would the government issue a high-level requirement and let companies figure out how to implement it, or would it identify a specific implementation for everyone to adopt?

Burrell suggested that, at the end of the day, law enforcement really wants access to plaintext, and he noted that the vast diversity of systems in use makes it difficult to specify exactly how this would be implemented.

A second key set of questions, Green said, relates to responsibility:

1. Who is responsible when things go wrong?
2. What happens when escrow keys are stolen or someone finds a vulnerability?

Picking up on this point later, Ball suggested that law enforcement would need to be held accountable for any failures that result from a key escrow system.

Turning to the more technical aspects of the question, Green suggested that abuse detection should be considered an important requirement. As Gillmor mentioned, it is valuable to be able to detect a breach and stop further damage, even if you can't always prevent the breach in the first place.

A related question is whether government actors would need only prospective capabilities—for example, the ability to decrypt future communications under a wiretap warrant—or also retrospective capabilities, such as the ability to retrieve past messages sent by a suspect in a terrorist attack. Green said it is unlikely that an exceptional access system would be able to both provide retrospective capabilities and detect abuse, although abuse detection may be possible in a system that only supports prospective decryption. To do so, one would have to have a design in which there is a master key that can be sent to a target's phone to cause all subsequent communications to be encrypted in a different way that would allow exceptional access.

To this point, Littlehale said retrospective exceptional access is not currently the highest priority for state and local law enforcement. Most companies have business reasons to access their own historical data and will respond to legal demands for whatever they possess. Although it might become a problem in the future if companies were to change their practices, he said it is not currently a major impediment. He emphasized that a much bigger problem is the devices and communication systems that are designed such that even the manufacturer cannot access their stored data or communication streams. Prompted by a follow-up question from Green, Littlehale later added that if the market were to move in a direction where cloud backups are also encrypted under user control, law enforcement would consider the ability to decrypt that information a far higher priority.

Picking up on this point later, Bankston suggested that approaches like that proposed in the Feinstein-Burr bill, which would require entities with the ability to encrypt to also retain the capability to decrypt, would essentially outlaw perfect forward secrecy, a technology coming into widespread use with which communications are encrypted with keys that are thrown away after use, so that if adversaries were to gain the keys for one TLS session, they would still lack the keys for other TLS sessions. Thus, if adversaries were able to gain access to a device, they would not be able to decrypt communications recorded in the past.

Burrell said that in his view, law enforcement wants both prospective and retrospective capabilities. In a communications system with perfect forward secrecy, one can still wait for the data in motion to become stored data when received, and access it then. Burrell also raised the point that timing is a consideration. On a mobile device, for example, how long are the data effectively stored, and how does that compare to how long the data are of value to law enforcement? Green replied that, ultimately, decisions about encryption and access must be made before the data are created. Under the assumption that anyone could become a suspect at some point in the future, if access to their data is desired, then that decision would have to be applied uniformly to everyone. This, in his view, would undoubtedly affect the security of the system.

Rescorla raised the question of whether it is a requirement that one must be able to detect when someone is not using escrowed encryption, arguing that determined adversaries—especially in the counterterrorism context—will use non-escrowed encryption and that it is not practical to detect when adversaries do so.

Littlehale noted that there may well be things law enforcement desires that are either not technically feasible or beyond what the public is comfortable entrusting to law enforcement. It may be that only incremental changes are possible. Given that law enforcement faces real barriers now and will likely face more of them in the future, he suggested that the most important thing is for these barriers to be understood and appreciated so that society can make its decisions in an informed way. Audience member Anand Gupta, from Harvard University and Palantir Technologies, suggested it would be useful, in the case of a large number of sometimes conflicting desires and requirements, to prioritize their relative importance.

Exploring a "k out of n" Solution

Lampson discussed his ideas for a system design that would allow exceptional access while providing reasonable security. He began by pointing out that although exceptional access necessarily makes a system less secure, it is quite possible that the reduction in security could be kept to a minimum such that the level of security could remain acceptable. He asserted that a k out of n model could provide such a solution. In this type of system, the encryption key is itself encrypted with a set of "sealing keys," for which a set of matched "unsealing keys" is created and given to trusted escrow agents. The escrowed encryption keys are broken into a number of pieces, n, and a certain number of them, k, must be combined in order to unlock the encryption.

Lampson identified two key weaknesses in such a system: First, one must determine what the sealing keys are—a configuration problem—and second, one must trust the escrow agents, which requires that technical bugs be eliminated from the escrow agent computer systems and, ultimately, involves trusting the people and institutions that operate each escrow agent. While acknowledging that such a scheme undoubtedly could be compromised, Lampson argued that such risks pale in comparison to the overall context and scale of existing security problems. He said the main counterargument he can envision relates to the policy issues articulated by Ball—namely, that the gain from an exceptional access system would not be worth the associated risks. From a practical standpoint, he added that it seems indubitable that countries like China and Russia are going to mandate exceptional access, including for American-made products sold in those countries.

Green commented that it is unlikely that such a system could be properly verified. Although certain types of programs are now formally verified in a research setting, he said that software engineers who would actually be building such a system "just don't speak that language." As a result, he said, any system built would likely have the same kinds of vulnerabilities that have been seen before. And while Green believed that it might be possible to find some number, k, of trustworthy organizations to serve as escrow agents, somewhere down the line, the systems they use to hold the escrowed keys will almost certainly share some common software. It is those pieces of software that Green believes would be the point where breaches occur and compromise the system.

Reiterating a previous point, Blaze reminded attendees that any such key escrow scheme would have to be robust against an attack by a nation-state, which is a significant risk, particularly for "important users" such as components of the national infrastructure that are critical for the U.S. economy and national security. In addition, unlike a system designed to protect seldom-used information, such as nuclear launch codes, for example, the exceptional access systems for the purposes being envisioned would have to be used every time there is a wiretap approval—perhaps on the order of once per hour or once per 15 minutes—yet provide security that is robust enough to deflect an adversary that is perhaps as sophisticated as the NSA. Landau reported that the number of federal and state wiretaps issued in 2014 was reported by the U.S. courts to be 3,554.[4]

In this vein, Rescorla noted that in addition to accommodating frequent access, it might be necessary to allow a large number of jurisdictions to have independent access. Lampson and Landau suggested that the mechanics of the institutions responsible for running the escrow agencies would require careful consideration and that keys would not be handed out at the level of every police department.

Landau wondered whether it matters if the escrow system uses off-the-shelf or specially developed communication software. While acknowledging that both approaches have downsides, Lampson reiterated that the relative risk of this system compared to what we have now is still minor. The larger threat, he emphasized, would be use of flawed methods to configure the sealing keys, which could put the sealing keys in the hands of adversaries. Green concurred with this point, citing as an example a configuration problem that resulted in a significant security vulnerability in Juniper network devices. But although the configuration challenge is a significant one, he expressed his belief that it might be solved but was not confident of this.

Sherman weighed in to urge caution, citing as a fundamental risk the increased complexity that a k out of n approach adds to a system: "We were all brought up to think that complexity is the enemy of security," he said. Pointing to largely offline, paper-based identification number storage systems of certain financial institutions as an example of a design that is compromised only rarely, he noted that any system in which we must store both data and keys online is, by nature, going to be more vulnerable than a system for which this information is not accessible via the Internet. LaMacchia expanded on this point, noting that "what we know about security for high-value assets is: We want stuff offline." Indeed, he said, some of Microsoft's cryptographic assets that are protecting high-value items involve keys that have both online and offline aspects. However, given the operational requirements currently envisioned for an exceptional access system, he said that such a system would likely need to be online.

---

[4] U.S. Courts, *Wiretap Report 2014*, last updated on December 31, 2014, http://www.uscourts.gov/statistics-reports/wiretap-report-2014.

Participants discussed how the *k* out of *n* approach might be tested experimentally and how its security risks could be better understood by examining existing systems that use a similar scheme. Lampson suggested one approach would be to develop the system and then offer a $5 million prize to anyone who can break it. Donner and Rescorla pointed to the signing of the Domain Name System's (DNS's) root server credentials as an example of a *k* out of *n* system. A key difference in the DNS case is that the keys are not stored in network-accessible systems, and the people holding portions of the key must gather physically. This approach is very expensive, making it impractical as a template for an exceptional access system that must be used frequently.

Rescorla described his main concerns about the *k* out of *n* scheme as relating to management of the system once it is built, although he also noted that the code itself would be difficult to write, and there would likely be many defects in implementation. "We are nowhere near having the ability to have a complete system which would have high confidence and security from the ground up," he said.

Gillmor pointed out that the use of *k* out of *n* schemes for signing authorities like the DNSSEC (Domain Name System Security Extensions) root zone signing keys, as distinct from decryption keys that would be necessary for an exceptional access mechanism, provides an opportunity for detecting a compromise, because the signatures must be distributed to an intended victim for theft of a signing key to be useful. The signing keys themselves can be kept secret, but victims who store or publish copies of the signatures that they receive could eventually be able to detect that the signing key was misused because they can see an artifact of its use. On the other hand, if an encryption key is compromised, it can be used in secret to decrypt captured ciphertext without raising any flags. Another important consideration, Gillmor added, is timing and maintainability. Many encryption systems protect data that need to be kept secret for an undetermined amount of time. For a *k* out of *n* system or any other system that provides an exceptional access mechanism to allow access to such information, it must be secure and function properly over the sensitive lifetime of the data encrypted using it. This is a significantly harder problem than seeking a short-term or revocable solution.

One final problem raised by LaMacchia is that securing any single environment is difficult, and in the *k* out of *n* scheme, one must secure *n* systems in parallel and maintain the security of all the other systems, even if one should fail. This increases the scale of the problem, and LaMacchia cautioned about underestimating the difficulties of physically securing that many components.

The Role of Hardware

Turning to other potential options, Littlehale questioned whether requiring physical access to the device in question would make a difference. Lampson suggested the security risks could be reduced by keeping the escrowed keys, sealed by the keys of the various escrow authorities, on the device rather than sending them to the authorities. Then an attacker would need both the device and the cooperation of *k* escrow authorities to release the escrowed key, rather than just the latter. In addition, this approach no longer depends on being able to reliably deliver the sealed key over the Internet.

Returning to this topic later, Bankston pointed out that while it may on the surface seem like requiring physical access to the device would help to contain security vulnerabilities, it is feasible in some countries for the government to seize a large number of phones, thus allowing those governments to steal encryption keys on a large scale. Lampson countered that a government like that of China would be more apt to mandate exceptional access than to gain access by physically seizing millions of phones. This sparked further debate concerning how a company like Apple might respond if mandated to provide exceptional access to the U.S. and/or the Chinese government. Bankston held that if the United States mandates such access, China will most certainly do so as well.

With regard to the need for law enforcement to access information on encrypted devices, Blaze said the question becomes whether the cost of creating the infrastructure necessary for access would exceed the cost of developing other methods law enforcement could use to gain access—for example, reverse-engineering the hardware. In this way, it becomes an economic question as well as a security question, and the economic component would be felt especially acutely by local law enforcement bodies.

The Feasibility of Segmenting by User

The discussion turned to the feasibility of segmenting exceptional access, but by user instead of by sector or technological layer, as had been discussed in Session 2.

Littlehale questioned whether every smartphone must be engineered to withstand an attack from a nation-state adversary. Several participants observed that the idea of creating "more secure" and "less secure" hardware or software is not generally a viewpoint supported by industry. LaMacchia responded that as a Microsoft cryptographer he works under an explicit directive to give the strongest protection to all users and assume a nation-state level threat for all products. Looking toward the long term, Microsoft implements this by adopting approaches like perfect forward secrecy. Rescorla concurred, characterizing the notion of providing good security for some users and bad security for others as "extremely unpleasant" from the perspective of a software or hardware manufacturer. If users have to go to extra effort to get strong security, the vast majority will not bother and will find themselves with weak protection.

LaMacchia added that it cannot be assumed that a device sold to an American user will only be operated in the United States. High-value targets, such as company CEOs and indeed anyone doing business internationally, may need strong encryption to defend against nation-state adversaries when traveling to other countries. Bankston later built on this point, noting that often the point of the attack is not to access an individual's information but to use the compromise of an individual's system as a platform from which to attack the valuable information of others. In that sense, he said, it is reasonable to think about hardening the entire "ecosystem" against adversaries such as China or Russia.

Bolstering the case that all users deserve strong encryption, Sherman pointed out that many strong cyber adversaries come not from the realm of nation-states but from technically sophisticated criminal networks seeking to steal people's money. The targets of such attacks are not limited to high-profile or necessarily high-value individuals or organizations.

Raising another potential downside of segmented encryption, Blaze noted that the current technology industry is built on the idea of general-purpose platforms that are controlled by easily loaded software. Somehow restricting this system by implementing architectures that would disallow user-supplied encryption could have serious economic ramifications. Tribble clarified this point by emphasizing that a motivated person could always find a way to load software implementing such encryption onto a device. In addition, he said it is likely unwise to try to segment exceptional access based on a distinction between hardware and software, particularly in the context of regulation, because the hardware-software boundary tends to shift over time.

The Government's Technical Resources: Lawful Hacking and Other Considerations

At several points throughout the workshop, participants considered what role the government's own technical expertise and resources should play in addressing the challenge of encryption—for example, through lawful hacking. They also considered how the technology industry and its security solutions bolster the security of the government itself as well as other ways to improve the government's access to information in the absence of an exceptional access mechanism.

Donner asked whether there are sufficient skills and technical resources in the law enforcement community to make use of this approach. Having the requisite skills in house can ensure that devices are handled correctly in circumstances such those that transpired in San Bernardino. Although such an approach will not always provide access to all the data from sophisticated criminals, it could give law enforcement more capabilities, at least against less sophisticated criminals.

Littlehale suggested that a regime based on massively up-staffed technical capabilities in the law enforcement and national security communities, even as industry continues to strengthen security, would create a situation where the United States is simultaneously devoting significant resources to improving security, on the one hand, and finding ways to compromise it, on the other. Moreover, if the government spends $5 million to find a vulnerability it can use, is it expected to then share it with the software creator so that it can be patched, only to require the government to spend another $5 million to find a vulnerability in the patch? Blaze responded that in some ways, building up the government's hacking capabilities will be feasible and indeed necessary, but not universally. Given that adversaries will in any case seek to bypass exceptional access mechanisms, lawful hacking will inevitably be needed even if there is a mechanism for exceptional access. If exceptional access is not given, he said, it certainly would require much greater investment by law enforcement.

Burrell weighed in on this matter, noting that lawful hacking is extremely complex due to the "vast universe" of devices and systems law enforcement would need to develop the capability to hack, and owing to the fact that those devices and systems have increasingly short life spans. In addition, the costs would comprise not only the direct cost of the experts working on this issue, it would also comprise the opportunity costs of removing those experts from other jobs and pulling resources from other tasks. Given all of this and the fact that law enforcement would be expected to reveal the vulnerabilities uncovered in the course of investigations to support cybersecurity aims, Burrell concluded by saying, "I just don't even see how that's even a feasible option."

Tribble suggested that better communication channels between companies and law enforcement could reveal currently unexploited resources that law enforcement could tap into even in the absence of an exceptional access system. Landau offered an anecdote to illustrate this point: A law enforcement organization complained that iMessage metadata sought for an investigation could not be accessed through communications providers like Verizon or AT&T. Instead, such information is held by Apple, where law enforcement never expected it to be. Given how rapidly the technology evolves, Tribble acknowledged that it is hard for law enforcement to keep up with what is actually available, and doing so is not something that law enforcement can be expected to do on its own. Cooperation from industry is important to building government capacity in this area, he suggested.

With regard to how government might take better advantage of available information, Burrell noted that just because more data or metadata are available does not mean they are accessible or necessarily useful to law enforcement. Sometimes, for example, they may be available but cannot be processed in a way that meets legal requirements for privacy or transparency. Sometimes those holding the data do not have a full understanding of what they are holding, Burrell said, and metadata are not standardized, so law enforcement does not always have a good idea of what it will receive when it asks for metadata. Moreover, just having metadata does not necessarily mean one has actionable information; sometimes there is a great deal of noise to sort through to find the useful pieces. Another key issue is timeliness: Burrell noted that it will not be workable for the government to spend 6 months hacking into a system if the information is needed in a matter of hours.

Landau pointed to the USA Freedom Act (P.L. 114-23), which caused the NSA to shift from collecting metadata to requesting metadata from individual communications firms. Burrell replied that the FBI does not have the same ability as the NSA to manage big data because it does not have the same business need for that capability. As a result, the company that holds the data or processes the communication would need to engineer special tools to transfer data to the FBI in a way that satisfies the FBI's legal requirements. He agreed with Landau's suggestion that requiring companies holding data to be able to provide them to law enforcement in a timely fashion would be an improvement over the current situation.

Littlehale added that law enforcement must know where data exist in order to request the data. If officers cannot get into a device, it would be impossible for them to find out if there is perhaps an unencrypted app or communications channel from which they could request data from the service provider. If the police were to try to get around this by prospectively sending a legal request for information, for example, to Google, they would be accused of fishing, he said. Pressing on this point, Landau asked whether law enforcement might make a request under 18 U.S. Code § 2703 (required disclosure of customer communications or records) to find out which communications came from the device. Littlehale said there are some technical challenges with such a request, some of which might be addressed by IPv6. Although it is possible in some cases to attribute activity to a particular device, in others it is not.

A related challenge, Littlehale said, is that law enforcement does not always receive instant responses from service providers. One potential avenue to explore is whether it would be possible to speed up these responses through automation. Another option for law enforcement is to open better communication channels with service providers to help its investigators understand which categories of data are available that they might not otherwise know about.

Building a More Productive Conversation

Even in the absence of any actual exceptional access mandate or policy, Landau noted that the government's posture toward end-to-end encryption could be affecting the technological landscape and wondered if it would be possible to work toward a different "default." For example, it is possible that government advocacy for exceptional access actually pushes the market more in the direction of user-controlled encryption.

Donner pointed out that the underlying driver stems in part from the fact that the Internet is constructed out of private components and open protocols—infrastructure the government doesn't control—and as such, the government is limited in its ability to protect citizens from bad actors operating online. If the government cannot adequately protect the network, then consumers have no choice but to protect themselves, and that in turn drives the trend toward end-to-end encryption.

Building on this point, Sherman pointed to the disclosures made by Edward Snowden as instrumental in raising interest in user-controlled encryption. However, given that government is asking for what it perceives as necessary to do its job, it is difficult to come up with anything the government could do to help the situation. Perhaps, he suggested, what is most needed is a more open and honest discussion between the government and its citizens. Littlehale concurred, noting that it would be useful to establish a less adversarial way of communicating about the issues. He reiterated the concern that a crisis situation can lead to hastily drawn-up legislation that does not necessarily achieve any of the desired goals.

6

Session 4. Technical and Policy Mitigations for Inaccessible Plaintext

The workshop's fourth session began with a presentation by Susan Landau. She covered a range of issues relevant to lawful hacking, including its benefits, its limitations, and the trade-offs it forces. Toward the end of her presentation, she also offered some solutions to the limitations as she sees them.

Orin Kerr then moderated a discussion covering a range of topics, including legal constraints and trends, considerations for the use of metadata, and the challenges and expectations for local, state, and federal law enforcement.

Landau began her remarks with an acknowledgment that although she had often disagreed with James Baker, the Federal Bureau of Investigation (FBI) general counsel, in the past, their views are moving into closer alignment. Indeed, he had said on the workshop's first day many of the same things she had planned to say in her presentation. One of the beliefs that they have in common, she said, is that the debate over encryption is not merely about privacy versus security but about privacy *and* security and how the two goals relate to law enforcement's ability to conduct investigations. Security is at the heart of both sides of the debate.

THE THREAT OF CYBERCRIME

Landau noted that cybercrime has topped the U.S. Worldwide Threat Assessment list in both 2015 and 2016.[1] Although domestic cyberattacks from international actors are not common currently, she cautioned that they could increase. Iran and North Korea, for example, do not have the same international constraints suppressing such attacks as China and Russia do. As an example, she said, a small, relatively unimportant dam in Westchester County, New York State, was hacked by Iranians in 2013. The attack itself was not particularly dangerous, Landau said—the worst that could have happened was that a few house basements could have been flooded—but it was an example of the type of attacks and attackers that might be faced in the future.

This type of threat means that not only do we need secure communications (the central issue in the first "Crypto War" 20-30 years ago), but we also need secure devices, Landau said. She posited that smartphones are the best forms of secure authentication and observed that companies like Google and Facebook have been using smartphone-based, two-factor authentication for their employees and customers. Government agencies also use phones for secure authentication, and Landau emphasized that if such phones themselves are made less secure, that makes them a less secure authenticator.

---

[1] J.R. Clapper, 2016, "Worldwide Threat Assessment of the U.S. Intelligence Community," https://www.dni.gov/files/documents/SASC_Unclassified_2016_ATA_SFR_FINAL.pdf.

TRENDS IN WIRETAPPING

To understand the scale at which mitigation is needed, Landau cited several pieces of data from the 2014 U.S. *Wiretap Report*,[2] the most recent report released as of the workshop date. Title III wiretapping covers electronic communication surveillance of criminals, and the report lists a range of information for these wiretaps, including who the district attorney was, who the judge was, how many incriminating conversations were logged, and how many arrests and convictions were made. Since 2000, the report has also listed the number of cases in which encryption was encountered in a wiretapped conversation. Unfortunately, it does not indicate whether a conviction was reached *because* of a wiretap, which would be virtually impossible to discern because of all the other factors juries must consider in addition to the content of the wiretap when deciding a case.

Despite that drawback, Landau said, the report offers useful data, particularly with regard to trends. In 2014, there were approximately 3,500 Title III wiretap requests, 1,300 from federal law enforcement and 2,300 from state and local law enforcement. Of the 3,500 requests, 3,400 were for mobile devices. This number is important to keep in mind, Landau said, because a mobile phone is more than just a phone. It tracks a user's location and much more information, some of which is not stored on the phone itself. It's an incredibly rich data source, as law enforcement is well aware. The data available from smartphones have placed surveillance in a new era, Landau averred, yet smartphones were adopted so quickly that society, Congress, and law enforcement may not have a fully developed understanding of how the situation has fundamentally changed.

Of the 3,500 wiretaps requested, 3,200 were for narcotics investigations. The rest relate to an assortment of other crimes, such as homicide, assault, and kidnapping. Landau mentioned kidnapping specifically because crimes against children are often cited in the context of these debates, but wiretaps are very rarely used in kidnapping (the number is usually about four per year), likely because investigators typically don't know who has the child. Tapping the phones of the missing child's family members is known as a "consensual overhear" and does not require a wiretap or involve encryption.

Not every wiretap request is granted. Only 313 federal wiretaps were installed in 2014, far fewer than the number requested, Landau pointed out. Each one costs the federal government about $41,000, most of which is spent on "minimization"—that is, someone to monitor the wiretap and assess its content. Landau noted that the number of wiretaps requested at the federal level increased in the 1990s and 2000s, then dropped by about half in the late 2000s, before increasing again to current rate of some 1,300 per year. State and local requests are also increasing.

Landau reiterated the point made by other workshop participants that encryption is still a relatively rare element in wiretaps because if law enforcement believes there will be encryption on a phone, they do not bother requesting a wiretap. Obtaining a wiretap warrant is a much more complicated process than obtaining a regular warrant, and it is typically not considered worth the time if a line is encrypted.

The increasing rate of state and local wiretap requests is significant, Landau noted, because those agencies have very different needs and resources than the federal agencies. Landau referred to James Burrell's statements concerning the FBI's Operational Technology Division (responsible for digital forensics, tactical operations, and other functions), which he noted has a budget in the hundreds of millions. But the FBI's budget for responding to the going dark problem is much smaller, Landau observed. Citing numbers provided to her by staff from the House Committee on the Judiciary, Landau said that the FBI's activities to respond to encryption and anonymization are carried out by 39 staff members (only 11 of whom are agents) and with a budget of $31 million (which may increase to $38 million in 2017, but without an increase in staff). These numbers are much smaller than people may assume, Landau pointed out, and state and local police are most likely spending even less.

During the discussion portion of this session, Burrell clarified that the budget and personnel figures Landau cited for going dark activities were from a budget request and did not necessarily reflect what the FBI or other federal, state, or local agencies actually spent on these activities. As for the personnel, Burrell declined to say whether the numbers she cited were correct. Landau clarified that those figures were the best that House Judiciary Committee staff, who twice tried to clarify this issue with the FBI, could provide. She argued that that kind of

---

[2] U.S. Courts, *Wiretap Report 2014*, last updated on December 31, 2014, http://www.uscourts.gov/statistics-reports/wiretap-report-2014.

information should be made public. In response, Burrell noted that the metrics are in a state of flux, which makes it difficult to quantify the level of effort required to respond to the going dark challenge.

Continuing with her presentation, Landau said that in addition to small budgets, another impediment to investigations is the wide variety of phones. In 2011, before there even were encrypted phones, Landau learned from Mark Marshall, the president of the International Association of Chiefs of Police, that the police's biggest difficulty was the variety of the devices people use. According to Landau, he said law enforcement does not have the resources to penetrate all the different operating systems they encounter in investigations. Landau wondered how local police might handle a fully encrypted phone today, given the technological changes of the past 5 years.

LAWFUL HACKING

Citing a paper she coauthored,[3] Landau turned to the topic of lawful hacking. She noted that the FBI first started its lawful hacking program in the early 2000s and has created several technologies to facilitate it. She described lawful hacking as a multistep process. First, agents obtain a court order to penetrate the device and determine the operating system and applications (and which versions of each) the device uses. Then, a second court order is needed for agents to actually exploit a vulnerability to install their surveillance software. Some devices are harder to hack than others, depending on how up-to-date and secure a user keeps it. The processes used to obtain the warrants needed to pursue lawful hacking are important, she emphasized. Some cases have been thrown out because the FBI didn't have the necessary two warrants.

Sometimes agents are able to exploit well-known security vulnerabilities, but sometimes they must purchase such knowledge. Landau said that a National Security Agency (NSA) employee once told her that any laptop could be hacked if the hacker wanted to do it badly enough. The San Bernardino iPhone hack brought that notion into the public consciousness.

Landau also noted that lawful hacking has to be particularized to each device. That makes it fundamentally different from previous wiretapping techniques such as alligator clips (surveillance equipment connecting a phone to a listening device, used in the 1930s) or wiretapping done under the Communications Assistance for Law Enforcement Act (CALEA, which uses a standardized wiretap interface and has the cooperation of the telecommunications provider). However, Landau emphasized that vulnerabilities will always exist. Decades ago, Fred Brooks wrote that long, complex programs will always have problems,[4] and today's programs are notably longer and more complex than ever before. Modern operating systems and applications are 10 times larger than the largest system from the time of the Orange Book (a Department of Defense standard for evaluating the effectiveness of computer security)[5] about 20 years after Brook's book. Eliminating bugs is a long, slow task, Landau said, and has not yet been accomplished.

Vulnerabilities are also a moving target. Once the vulnerability used for the exploit is patched, a substitute needs to be found. Landau noted that the vulnerabilities that enable hacks can last a very long time. At last count, several years ago, the average was 312 days. This is important to keep in mind, Landau said, because when the FBI hacks in, it is liable to be able to use it for a while.

Lawful hacking costs vary. Using a well-known vulnerability could be nearly free, but finding a new one could cost from $10,000 to upwards of $1 million, as in the San Bernardino case, said Landau.

Overall, Landau argued that lawful hacking is a necessary solution. The most sophisticated criminals, such as the Mexican criminal syndicate known as Los Zetas, have extremely good security. In order to investigate such criminals, the FBI needs particularized solutions. Furthermore, as encryption-secured devices become increasingly ubiquitous, the FBI will need particularized solutions every time it conducts an investigation, regardless of the sophistication of the target.

---

[3] S.M. Bellovin, M. Blaze, S. Clark, and S. Sandau, 2013, "Lawful Hacking: Using Existing Vulnerabilities for Wiretapping on the Internet," Privacy Legal Scholars Conference, June, available at Social Science Research Network, http://papers.ssrn.com/sol3/papers.cfm?abstract_id=2312107.

[4] F.P. Brooks, Jr., 1975, *The Mythical Man-Month: Essays on Software Engineering*, Addison-Wesley, Reading, Mass.

[5] U.S. Department of Defense, 1983, The Trusted Computer System Evaluation Criteria.

THE ROLE OF METADATA

Landau then turned to the issue of communications metadata, offering several examples of different ways metadata have been used in criminal investigations. While it once took the U.S. Marshals Service an average of 44 days to track fugitives, Landau noted that with cell phone surveillance, now it takes only 2 days.

Landau provided another example from 2009, when Boston police were able to catch the "Craigslist killer" after analyzing closed-circuit television images and cell phone records from the hotel where the murder occurred. A 2008 Drug Enforcement Agency (DEA) investigation offers another example. In that case, the targets were constantly switching cell phone ownership, making it impossible for the agents to obtain wiretaps. However, after being granted location information for the phones, they were able to crack the case.

Landau noted that she only learned about the DEA story from Baker's 2010 testimony about the case to the Senate Judiciary Committee.[6] In her view, this underscores that there is very little publicly available data about *how* investigations are run. Although it is understandable that the FBI cannot always share its methods, she posited that such information would be useful in the context of this discussion. Without the appropriate data, Landau stated, technologists, academics, and the government are unable to have a reasonable discussion about the trade-offs that are being made. When the first Crypto Wars were taking place, she said, the *Wiretap Report*[7] data were very helpful. Right now, there are no public data about which techniques the government uses to conduct investigations, such as metadata, lawful hacking, or tools used to track online trafficking of child pornography—nor do we know how effective those techniques are.

THE INTERNET OF THINGS

Building on the discussion from a previous session, Landau highlighted the additional challenges presented by the proliferation of the Internet of Things (IoT). The concern is not about the security of our refrigerators or toasters, she said, but rather about the information that such devices can unwittingly transmit about their user, such as when they are home or how many people live in a household. The IoT can also offer more avenues into a secured network. She cited as an example the view of Rob Joyce, head of the NSA's Tailored Access Operations Unit and known as the nation's "hacker-in-chief," who told the audience at the USENIX Enigma conference in January 2016 that the most useful information to hackers today is the login credentials of systems administrators and others with a high level of network access.

POTENTIAL SOLUTIONS

Looking forward, Landau offered some solutions to the problems she outlined. First and most important, she suggested that the FBI and its Going Dark program should be operating with far more resources. Cyberthreats are real, Landau emphasized, and systems must be secured against them. This budget would be a necessary expense. Computer bits comprise—and compromise—much of the world's plans, software, and knowledge. Those bits are easily stolen, Landau said, making it critical to secure login credentials and communication. In this arena, she said, law enforcement is "badly outgunned."

Second, she argued that a Vulnerabilities Equities Process (VEP) should be established for law enforcement. Landau referred to Chris Inglis's comments at the workshop about the VEP and how the NSA reports 93 percent of the vulnerabilities, domestic or international, that it finds (although it is not known how quickly they are reported). The FBI's unlocking of the 2015 San Bernardino shooting suspect's iPhone disturbed Landau, she said, because they paid a third party to do it without handing the vulnerability they exploited over to Apple. The bureau cannot tell Apple how to fix it (leaving aside the question of whether it should hand over a vulnerability it paid $1 mil-

---

[6] Statement of James A. Baker, Associate Deputy Attorney General, U.S. Department of Justice, before the Senate Judiciary Committee, September 22, 2010, https://www.justice.gov/sites/default/files/testimonies/witnesses/attachments/09/22/10/09-22-10-baker-electronic-comm-privacy-act.pdf.

[7] U.S. Courts, *Wiretap Report 2014*, 2014.

lion for when Apple had no "bug bounty" to pay for it themselves), yet it does know that it affects the phones of millions of people. Landau called this situation "appalling."

A third possible solution is the creation of an official policy of information sharing to assist state and local law enforcement agencies, which are having a much harder time than the FBI even as they are filing more wiretap requests than the federal government. Information sharing, perhaps through regional centers, could help.

More education and better communication could also make a significant impact, Landau said, while being relatively easy to accomplish. Landau praised Baker for his frequent engagement in dialogue and listening on these issues with researchers and academics.

Part of the problem, Landau reiterated, is that the world has shifted, yet law enforcement does not fully understand those shifts. For example, investigators did not realize that iMessage metadata are stored with Apple, rather than with the telecommunications provider. She suggested that officers need to feel comfortable asking for assistance when they run into technology they do not understand, so that their understanding can grow. Companies do cooperate with law enforcement, even without a legal requirement to do so—for example, by voluntarily scanning image hashes to detect known images of child pornography. Although there has been tension over the San Bernardino case, Landau has also seen promising examples of cooperation between the FBI and private companies in the computer industry and believes that there could be more.

Although the variety of communications metadata formats is a problem for law enforcement, Landau said, the research community has tackled similar problems before, as exemplified by an article by Kathleen Fisher and Robert Gruber[8] about dealing with unstructured data. Landau asserted that a technological advisory board could help the FBI leverage this sort of work.

In closing, Landau asked the group to look at encryption and lawful hacking in another way—as cost shifting. Moving away from easier wiretapping secures the general public but makes wiretaps more expensive. Expensive wiretaps, however, have always been supported in the past, she said. Supporting them now would mean significantly expanding the FBI's going dark program as well as establishing better mechanisms to aid state and local law enforcement.

DISCUSSION

Orin Kerr moderated an open discussion, taking up many of the points Landau presented in her talk. The discussion is arranged here by topic; the order of the contributions does not necessarily match the order in which items were discussed at the workshop.

Unintended Outcomes and the Balance Between Legal and Technical Protections

Kerr expressed his belief that the responses to—and investment in—the Going Dark program relate to an equilibrium between legal and technical protections. When there are more technical protections on data, he suggested, the court will require less legal protection. If technology weakens data security, the courts tend to step in to increase legal protections.

In the current encryption landscape, he argued that that the technological protection will likely grow, and so the courts will give technology less legal protection. He cited as an example the treatment of metadata. Metadata are especially tricky because the courts are not sure if it they are covered by the Fourth Amendment. He believes that as encryption gets stronger and more widespread, making investigations more difficult, the courts will respond by limiting the constitutional protection for metadata. He challenged attendees to consider whether that is a tradeoff we are comfortable with. In response to this idea, Bankston posited that there are many areas where protection would not be *lost*, because the item or data type (such as metadata) is already unprotected, although he declined to take a firm stance on the legal/technical balance Kerr had suggested.

---

[8] K. Fisher and R. Gruber, 2005, "PADS: A Domain-Specific Language for Processing Ad Hoc Data," *PLDI '05: Proceedings of the 2005 ACM SIGPLAN Conference on Programming Language Design and Implementation*, Association for Computing Machinery, pp. 295-304.

Kerr raised another, perhaps more troubling, prospect. Before iOS 8, the government could obtain a warrant and easily decrypt a phone's data. Given the difficulty of opening a post-iOS 8 phone or a similarly protected device, investigators are now forced to turn to other methods. Kerr pointed to a case in the Third Circuit Court of Appeals of a former police officer allegedly dealing in child pornography who would not divulge his computer passcode; he was found in contempt of court and jailed until he discloses the password. Kerr noted that it is quite possible for someone to withhold a passcode purposefully, but it is also possible for someone to genuinely forget it, and this is left to a judge to decide. If "failure to decrypt your device" leads to indefinite jail time, Kerr asked, is that an outcome we are willing to accept?

Matt Blaze suggested that the risk of such outcomes will lessen as the technology continues to evolve. The actual encryption keys are generally derived from passwords and pass phrases, so it is rare for someone to have direct knowledge of the encryption key to unlock stored data. Moreover, because people can't remember long sequences of numbers, passcodes that humans can remember are highly vulnerable to a computerized search. He said future approaches are more likely to use passcodes that unlock a security module that actually holds the security key, which is either within the security module or deleted immediately after use. Thus, if law enforcement cannot force a suspect to divulge the passcode, investigators can instead attack the security module to extract the key.

Weighing in later in the discussion, Bankston argued that this is clearly an issue of due process and one that he believes the courts can adjudicate. It belongs in that realm, he reasoned, and not in the discussion about encryption, where decisions are being made that could affect the information security of billions of people. He suggested that far fewer people are likely to be detained for refusing to provide passcodes than are likely to be adversely affected by insecure phones.

Daniel Kahn Gillmor suggested that an important aspect of this scenario is that the ability of investigators to enter the suspect's computer depends on the suspect actively divulging his passcode. On the other hand, if law enforcement can exploit a vulnerability to get in, a suspect would not necessarily know that his or her encryption has been broken. Gillmor argued that targets of investigations should be notified when the government breaks into their software or device through lawful hacking. Taking a lesson from wiretapping procedure, Landau replied that the law requires that a person wiretapped in a law enforcement investigation be notified 90 days after the tap has ended.[9] For an intelligence wiretap, the target is notified only if content from it is used in court.

Another factor that is potentially more disruptive to law enforcement than encryption is file deletion, Blaze pointed out. There are, of course, perfectly legitimate reasons to delete files, such as when someone wants to sell their computer to someone else, but erasing or overwriting files containing evidence of criminal activity is very common. Nevertheless, there has been little discussion about restricting such behavior or weakening deletion capabilities.

Gillmor reiterated his view that these questions will continue to come up, because all of the proposed systems for exceptional access are still bypassable, and some passwords will be unbreakable. People will always want to protect their data, and there will always be software to enable that. Even the threat of indefinite jail time will not be effective against the world's worst criminals, he argued, because they will always find a way to protect their data.

Richard Littlehale countered that most criminals are not very sophisticated, so even a bypass-able system could be useful. In addition, he suggested that perhaps technological trends such as biometrics could help law enforcement avoid indefinite jailing of suspects who refuse to give up their passcodes. Although not a perfect solution, a method of unlocking a phone that could be compelled without undue harm to its owner could be very helpful, he said.

Exploring Divergent Perspectives on Metadata

Landau noted that in the communications world, there has so far been a clear distinction between message content and message metadata. Metadata, which include information on dialing, signaling, routing, and addressing, have generally not been well protected and can be obtained via subpoena. However, when Landau and her colleagues looked deeper into the issue in the modern context, they found that it was technically very muddled and that there was a vast middle area between content and metadata. Sometimes, what is not itself content can still be *revealing* of content.

---

[9] 18 USC Sec. 2518(8)(d).

On the theory that if we have greater technical protection on our phones it would lead to less legal protection in other areas, Kerr suggested that the courts could wind up defining all those data in the middle as metadata and give the government access to them. Although the debate is often framed as privacy versus security, he said that he sees it more as about different kinds of security, different kinds of privacy, and different civil liberties.

Reiterating a point discussed in the workshop's third session, Landau pointed out that because phones contain so much more data than they did 10 or 20 years ago, they on balance still provide investigators with a tremendous amount of material. Kerr countered that the courts could argue that that material is also not protected by the Fourth Amendment. Such an outcome would give everyone less protection, he argued, because the courts would be saying that the government can access data that are not on the device, plus they can even access the device itself with the threat of jail time, as previously discussed. Kerr and Landau agreed that the distinction is between something that can be accessed easily or not accessed at all.

Pointing to the 2014 *Wiretap Report*,[10] Bankston noted that out of approximately 25 instances where encryption was detected, law enforcement was unable to extract plaintext only 4 times. Landau noted Bankston and Soltani's paper on *United States v. Jones*,[11] which Bankston described as underscoring the fact that as technology evolves, it is getting exponentially easier and cheaper for law enforcement to conduct surveillance. Gillmor emphasized the flip side of the trade-off Kerr posited: If the courts tend toward providing less protection for metadata, then technology will evolve to provide more. Noting that there are already messaging services that protect metadata, he cautioned that those who want less legal protection of metadata should be aware that they are encouraging stronger encryption technology overall. Gillmor then questioned whether Kerr's balance theory is right, noting that he has not seen an increase in legal protections for metadata even as people develop more technologies to curtail it. In response, Kerr noted some examples of protection of metadata, such as the California Electronic Consumer Protection Act, which requires a warrant for pursuing electronic surveillance and metadata warrant protections (several courts have stated that metadata are protected by the Fourth Amendment).

Burrell addressed some nuances related to the value and use of metadata in the law enforcement context. Although metadata format is not an issue for the FBI, he said, data management presents a far greater challenge. The growth of metadata has brought much more data to bear on every investigation, but he cautioned that that does not mean much of it is useful as evidence. Burrell said that the FBI has discussed metadata standards with various communications providers and metadata storage organizations, which are usually aware that their data could be useful to law enforcement. However, they do not all collect the same information, which is a key difference from the past. Building on this point, Landau pointed out that 30 years ago there was only one communications provider, whereas now there are multiple providers and multiple communication methods. Burrell concurred and noted that there are a number of providers now that, for various reasons, are not covered by CALEA. Despite a general perception that law enforcement always get the data they want, that is not actually the case, he said.

Landau reiterated the point that a technical advisory board could help the FBI identify and better utilize all the information channels available to it. Some companies are extremely good at instrumenting and measuring things, she said, and those skills could help the FBI.

Littlehale noted that a further complication in the use of metadata by law enforcement relates to the difference between knowing something and being able to prove it in court. The police may know *where* a phone was at a certain time, but it is extremely difficult to prove in court exactly *who* was holding that phone at the time, especially in the absence of video evidence or a direct observation of the event.

Phone-Based Authentication: Strengths and Weaknesses

Kerr returned to Landau's argument about the value of encryption for supporting smartphones as authenticators. In the physical world, he said, authentication standards are not very secure; a driver's license or the last four digits

---

[10] U.S. Courts, *Wiretap Report 2014*, 2014.

[11] K.S. Bankston and A. Soltani, 2014, "Tiny Constables and the Cost of Surveillance: Making Cents Out of *United States v. Jones*," *The Yale Law Journal Online*, Volume 123, January 9, http://www.yalelawjournal.org/forum/tiny-constables-and-the-cost-of-surveillance-making-cents-out-of-united-states-v-jones.

of a social security number are often accepted. In that context, he asked, why does phone authentication in particular require such strong security?

Landau replied that it is needed because of the scale of crime that digital platforms make possible. In the physical world, you are limited by how many humans can pull off a scheme such as a bank robbery. Online, many banks could be targeted simultaneously using machines. Even one phone that falls into the wrong hands—for example, when someone is separated from their phone during airport screening or in a confidential meeting—could offer an adversary important access points for valuable information or account credentials.

Kerr pointed out that the discussion was not whether certain "VIPs" need phones with good security, it's whether everyone should have them. The rule should be for everyone or for no one, he said. Given that, he asked, how much security would be needed to have secure authentication? Landau emphasized that in her view all consumer phones should have a high level of encryption. Many high-level government employees use consumer phones for secure authentication (sometimes in order to hide the fact that they are government employees, she noted), as do VIPs in many other industries.

Underscoring this point, Donner emphasized that government agencies and others are strongly dependent on consumer technology because history has proven that developing customized technology is a dead end. Because consumer technology is far more widely used than customized technology, companies like Apple and Google can take advantage of economies of scale. It is also far easier to find and fix bugs if millions of people are using your products. Gillmor added that using consumer devices for official work also requires far less training and is easier on users.

The Government's Responsibilities When Vulnerabilities Are Exposed

When the government hacks into a system, must it divulge the exploited vulnerability so it can be fixed? Given that if the FBI has found a vulnerability, criminals can too. Landau argued that the vulnerability must be disclosed to protect others using that software or device. This is an argument about security, she said, not privacy. One caveat, as mentioned in the lawful hacking paper cited above,[12] is that the obligation for immediate disclosure might be stronger in the context of law enforcement than in the context of national security, she said. This is because law-enforcement investigations are generally within the United States; therefore, a vulnerability that works for accessing one criminal's phone is likely to also be present in many other phones in use by legitimate users in the United States, she explained.

Picking up on topics raised earlier in the workshop, Kerr noted that disclosing vulnerabilities raises the cost of government hacking. Landau countered that when viewed in the context of the cost of cybercrime in the United States, a much higher budget for federal, state, and local law enforcement is justified. Furthermore, she said, if it takes an average of 312 days to fix a known vulnerability, then law enforcement should be able to use it much more than once, even after disclosure. In response to a question from Littlehale, several participants noted that the number of potential vulnerabilities in an operating system is essentially infinite.

Rescorla posited that lawful hacking presents a threat to others users of that software or hardware.

The longer a vulnerability is used by the government, the more likely it is that criminals will discover and exploit it. There are three primary ways in which government possession and use of a vulnerability increases the risk, Rescorla suggested. First, when the government uses the vulnerability, they are inherently disclosing it to their targets, who might discover how it works. Second, if the vulnerability is purchased rather than found by the government, it could be sold again to someone else. Third, if the government discloses vulnerability in court, then this information might leak. Any lawful hacking program needs to take these risks into account when crafting disclosure policies, he added.

Picking up on the question of whether and how an exploited vulnerability might be understood in the court system, Littlehale pointed to a criminal defendant's right to challenge the foundation of evidence offered against him or her. In some cases it may be that the defendant or the court will want to know exactly how the information was obtained or require proof that the information was not altered.

---

[12] S.M. Bellovin et al., 2013.

7

Wrap-Up Session

For the final session, Fred Cate wrapped up the workshop by giving each participant a final chance to add comments to the discussion. He invited them to address one or more of the following four questions:

- Is there anything that has not been said that you think needs to be said?
- Is there anything you have heard that has been particularly surprising?
- Do you have any broad suggestions for next steps?
- Do you have comments on whether the discussion that we have, which focused largely on law enforcement examples related to the technologies of encryption and their implications, can be applied in the national security environment, or whether there are special or distinct considerations in the national security environment that affect these technological questions?

In the following summary, participant comments are grouped by topic.

COSTS OF EXCEPTIONAL ACCESS

Kevin Bankston began the discussion by suggesting that there is a need to invest in law enforcement's technical capabilities. He said that a substantial policy and legal debate is necessary to define responsible, reasonable, and constitutional government hacking. He suggested that the United States can either invest hundreds of millions of dollars to update law enforcement's investigative capabilities for the 21st century or the economy can face a loss of billions of dollars if exceptional access is mandated for U.S. products. Susan Landau underscored Bankston's argument that Silicon Valley brings enormous value to the U.S. economy and national security alike, noting that the nation's defense organizations have relied heavily on commercial, off-the-shelf technology for the past 20 years and that these products have been critically important for national security. This, in Landau's view, supports the argument that device encryption should be as strong as possible. Bankston indicated his support for raising law enforcement's technological capabilities rather than diminishing the capabilities of technology for everyone.

Matt Blaze agreed with Bankston's comments from a technical perspective and posited that the costs of an exceptional access mandate would be enormous. He pointed to the 1990s, when a tremendous amount of effort spent trying to resolve this debate served as a distraction and discouraged the development of critical security infrastructure that could have prevented a large fraction of the digital crimes seen today. Standards, infrastructure, and products are not nearly as robust as they should be and could have been, in his view. He suggested that, if these same mistakes are repeated, the costs will be even higher, and that the stakes will continue to rise. He added that it is critically important to national security and to our public safety that the government not discourage, but instead encourage, the use of the most robust security technology for our increasingly digital world.

Daniel Kahn Gillmor echoed Blaze's sentiment on the significant downside of exceptional access. In his view, any benefits to law enforcement are likely to be small and diminishing, because such a system would undoubtedly be bypassable. Developers of encryption software are trying to provide better security for everyone by designing systems that minimize risk; any type of exceptional access, he emphasized, would increase risk. In his view, none of the proposed schemes could reliably distinguish between exceptional access for law enforcement and unauthorized access. He emphasized the importance of open discussion of security needs and looked to existing engineering communities that operate based on openness as one possible avenue for future discussions. Finally, Gillmor suggested that if the goal is increased security of communications for law-abiding citizens, security—and in particular strong cryptographic protections—should be enabled as a default setting.

Andrew Sherman asked how much of our economy we are willing to hand over to organized crime if we get security around lawful access wrong. He noted that security concerns are not just about foreign governments trying to hack into our systems, but also about criminals acting for financial gain.

Eric Rescorla added some perspective on software, pointing out that security has become a very high priority for software companies because of its importance to users. Encryption, which is one of the only tools that software companies have for addressing security, is increasingly expected by end users, he said, and consumer software will increasingly incorporate encryption features; any requirement for exceptional access would become a large burden because software companies must take on the responsibility of managing the systems and processes. Although this would be difficult enough for a large organization, it would be very difficult for the many very small companies or individuals who are app developers, owing to the relative ease of building software today, Rescorla observed. In addition, the availability of open-source software and operating systems would make it very hard to enforce compliance by app developers. The risk of losing control of an exceptional access asset is especially serious for communications applications compared to storage applications, he added, because communications could be remotely captured without a user's knowledge.

PRACTICAL CONSIDERATIONS

Orin Kerr predicted that exceptional access mandates are unlikely to happen. As reflected in the discussions at this workshop, there is a strong aversion to the idea of exceptional access in many communities, and from a more practical standpoint, it remains unclear what exceptional access mandates would look like and what the parameters would be.

Rescorla raised another, more specific practical impediment. Given that the best designs for providing exceptional access are escrow systems that, by design, involve long-term access (to provide retrospective access to data once they have been transmitted), not only must these assets be protected, but they must be protected in perpetuity. In many cases, this would involve keeping assets in escrow long after the company has gone out of business and ceased to provide any services to users.

Butler Lampson suggested that the best way to understand the practical feasibility and security implications of a key escrow system would be to build a test system and study it. He proposed using an approach similar to that used in the Defense Advanced Research Projects Agency's challenge competitions for self-driving cars and robotics. This could involve, for example, funding five or ten universities to build such a system and then offering a big prize for breaking it. Such an approach might cost $20 to $40 million dollars, and the results could add a lot of clarity to the discussion, he said.

At several points throughout the workshop, participants discussed the need for the law enforcement and national security communities to enhance their hacking capabilities, either as part of a "Plan A"—that is, alongside the development of an exceptional access scheme—or as a "Plan B"—the only viable option for accessing plaintext if exceptional access is not possible. Cate said that although this might be the inevitable, and perhaps right, thing to do, it could be difficult to sell the idea to policy makers and the public that the best solution is for companies to invest in building stronger and stronger encryption and then for government to invest more and more public money to try to break into it. He noted that it may be important to find a better way of talking about this idea to make it more palatable.

Taking a different perspective, Bankston suggested that such an approach could be considered a win-win situation. "I think that [it] is actually an appropriate use of government resources to both investigate a crime and then prevent many more crimes by getting the vulnerability patched," he said. Given that fighting cybercrime is also part of broader law enforcement goals, the security gained by allowing vulnerabilities to be patched should be factored into the cost/benefit analysis for lawful hacking.

The compelling arguments on both sides of discussions about encryption and lawful access make it increasingly important to find common ground rather than thinking in absolutes, said Cate. This requires not just thinking at the macro level but also, in very specific terms, about the choices that will have to be made in various situations. Decisions must be made, said Cate, yet it isn't clear who will make these decisions: Congress, courts, the market, or hackers? Could it be that law enforcement makes decisions because they have not been given any general guidance by Congress in this area? "We may not like the thought that there are decisions, but in the inevitability that there will be, I think it becomes increasingly important to say who makes them and based on what information and what values," said Cate.

Cate also echoed Lampson's point that it is important to recognize the intersections between technology, law, and politics. Bad things are going to happen, and political leaders often respond in ways that may not meet our definitions of what is rational or well thought out. The risk is that when a crisis or key event happens, the issues that have been talked about during this workshop in what Cate described as a "fairly erudite and high-flying manner" will be dealt with in a "fairly bold and brash manner." This means that not only should perfect, best, or ideal solutions be developed, but also "second best, and quick-and-dirty ways of dealing with issues on the fly." Recognizing that many of the technologists at the workshop feel that it would be impossible to mitigate all of the risks of encryption, Fred Chang pointed out that exogenous factors can sometimes force an issue, and thus it could be good to have already thought through the technology mitigations so that you are not scrambling to respond.

Referencing a paper from the literature on the economics of cybersecurity,[1] Chang said that the authors found a positive correlation between firms that had used encryption and the likelihood that there would be a reported data breach afterward. In other words, the probability of a data breach goes up after encryption is implemented, a counterintuitive finding. The authors speculated that perhaps the firms thought they were secure because they had encrypted then got careless. One take-home message from that anecdote is that some consequences may be counterintuitive, and some sort of technology forecasting could help us to understand and ward off unintended consequences.

GLOBAL DIMENSIONS OF ENCRYPTION AND ACCESS MECHANISMS

Kerr referred to earlier comments made by Chris Inglis and James Baker, who said that some form of international coordination about how to approach exceptional access mandates is necessary to make such strategies even remotely effective. He noted that this requirement significantly raises the level of difficulty of the task, making a solution even more unlikely. He shared his view that, in the event of a major terrorist attack, the government would be more likely to implement requirements that are just outside of exceptional access mandates, such as data retention requirements.

Brian LaMacchia pointed out that although implementing high-quality encryption is not trivial, the skill to create such implementations exists around the world. High-quality open-source encryption technology is available everywhere. He argued that any type of duty imposed on U.S. companies in terms of the software they write will put this software at a disadvantage relative to the rest of the world because people can acquire similar software overseas. LaMacchia said that there has already been what he views as an irrational shift away from cryptographic standards from the National Institute of Standards and Technology simply because they are U.S.-based. Moreover,

---

[1] A.R. Miller and C. Tucker, 2010, "Encryption and Data Loss," Workshop on the Economics of Information Security, http://www.econinfosec.org/archive/weis2010/papers/session1/weis2010_tucker.pdf.

users can circumvent controls through superencryption. Trying to block superencryption inevitably leads to bugs because it requires violating the abstractions one depends on when engineering complex yet trustworthy systems, LaMacchia observed.

Cate observed that if the vast majority of encryption software comes from overseas, and it is getting increasingly accessible and easy to use, then everyone could use software from someplace else, and U.S. regulations would have little impact. However, he noted that similar arguments could apply to a lot of other areas that the United States nonetheless chooses to regulate. For example, the United States imposes environmental regulations within its borders even though other nations take a different approach. He suggested that waiting on or expecting an international compact on encryption is unrealistic. While figuring out how to address the international challenge is beyond the scope of this workshop, it is directly relevant to the issues this workshop is charged with.

Drew Mitnick with Access Now suggested that, while countries such as China and Russia may pursue their own aims (which would likely include government back doors), a lot of other countries may look to the United States on this. He argued that the broader global impact of the U.S. policies under consideration needs to be kept in mind.

MEETING LAW ENFORCEMENT NEEDS

Richard Littlehale pointed out that if the national conversation concludes that exceptional access is not appropriate, then it will be necessary to figure out what alternative options can meet the needs of law enforcement. He suggested that a next step could be bringing law enforcement and technologists together for discussions within an academic or institutional setting akin to the present workshop. In such forums, the technical experts could offer their perspectives on alternative sources of the evidence that law enforcement needs, and law enforcement experts could share their perspective on the feasibility of those alternatives when understood in the context of the realities of the criminal justice system. Underscoring the value of such exchange, Littlehale emphasized that leaving technologists out of the discussion when laws are made can result in serious unintended consequences. He suggested that continuing to have calm, productive, and ongoing conversations could help avoid mandates that fail to either resolve problems or address stakeholder needs.

Kerr noted that it is helpful to keep in mind the three contexts in which the issues being debated and discussed arise: (1) national security intelligence, which gets the majority of the attention; (2) federal criminal law enforcement; and (3) state and local law enforcement. The best path forward must address the needs of all three at the same time, he said, but their needs are likely different. For example, the device encryption issue is primarily, but not exclusively, a criminal law issue at the federal, state, and local levels more than a national security issue.

Commenting on the recommendation to increase FBI funding for technical capabilities, specifically computer network exploitation, James Burrell reminded attendees that computer network exploitation is by no means a singular solution to this challenge. He noted that many discussions around law enforcement requirements focus on a particular problem or particular technical issue, while in reality, a typical investigation usually involves multiple challenges and thus brings more complexities. Burrell also emphasized the importance of scalability and timeliness to the FBI.

He added that FBI Director James Comey has been adamant about the FBI's greater engagement with academia and industry as well as other government agencies, in order to identify potential technical options and to facilitate a better understanding. He added that the FBI is interested in continuing these discussions outside of this particular forum. He also explained that the FBI has a technical advisory board that works with the FBI itself, other foreign governments, industry, and academia. The board identifies new technologies, examines their adoption and use by potential adversaries, and considers the implications for the FBI's own work.

Marc Donner suggested that a fair amount of the challenge faced by law enforcement stems not only from insufficient technological capabilities, but also from staff not having an appropriate level of training in how to handle technical assets and devices. Governance is going to be a key factor in solving this problem, he said, adding that the issue of governance extends far beyond the FBI and broadly into the law enforcement community.

Lampson proposed a possible solution for the budget and resource problems faced by law enforcement. A commercial or government-sponsored organization could bring together expertise so that anybody with a legitimate governmental need for lawful hacking could send that organization a seized smartphone and have the best available resources applied to cracking it. This, he suggested, would be preferable to fragmented efforts where no single entity has sufficient resources to succeed.

Bud Tribble said that much discussion of lawful hacking would be needed to arrive at an equities disclosure process that works across law enforcement. He also believes that an increased amount of funding and training by law enforcement, whether it is local, state, or federal, will help to increase the productivity of discussions between law enforcement, industry, and academia. He also said it was "pleasantly surprising" to hear more from government attendees regarding the issues of collective security versus individual security, instead of framing the issue as being about choices in business models.

Sherman pointed to a blog post by Columbia University computer scientist Steve Bellovin in July 2014, "What Spies Do,"[2] that summarizes some of the differences between the law enforcement sector and the national security sector, including places where behavior that is acceptable in one sector is totally unacceptable in the other because of differences in function, levels of proof required, and so forth. At a 90,000-foot level, Landau clarified that national security focuses on investigations, as opposed to collecting evidence, whereas law enforcement has to do both. Also, national security is largely focused outside the United States, while law enforcement is largely focused inside the country. These distinctions bring different needs in terms of the quality of the information and how it is obtained. These two areas also have important differences in the resources that are available to them. Finally, because of where national security and law enforcement activities are focused, she said that there is an argument for changing the Vulnerabilities Equities Process.

DISCLOSURE OF VULNERABILITIES

Several participants addressed the government's responsibilities when it discovers a vulnerability in the course of lawful hacking. Kerr noted that many of these issues are only starting to be considered. Given the great expenditure of resources involved in finding vulnerabilities, Kerr argued that it may be unlikely that those vulnerabilities will be routinely disclosed to private companies. He suggested that perhaps these questions might be dealt with using something similar to the Classified Information Procedures Act (P.L. 96-456, 94 Stat. 2025), an effort to deal with the potential disclosure of classified information in prosecutions in the court setting. He said the topic of vulnerabilities deserves more discussion and possibly its own workshop.

LaMacchia said that from a private sector standpoint, it is highly desirable for law enforcement to disclose any vulnerabilities it uncovers. It would put companies in a terrible position to be unable to act on a vulnerability that has been discovered. Landau said that in the context of national security, while she can see why U.S. companies would want to know about vulnerabilities, she also understands the logic of the argument that if there are very few users within the United States and many abroad, especially if they are targets of interest, it would be reasonable to delay informing the company.

Landau added that globalization and the Internet have drastically changed the world in the past 20 to 30 years, yet society and societal structures have not changed at the same pace. Referring to Kerr's earlier comment that if we are using a technology, we have to explain it to the courts, Landau asked, "Will we explain the vulnerabilities? How will we do that?" If the courts are to use evidence that stems from lawful hacking or related approaches, they will need to know something about how it works and whether or not there are potential errors in it.

THE USE OF METADATA

Tribble brought up the fact that with the increasing prevalence of user-controlled encryption comes an ever-increasing footprint of data that includes metadata, content, or something in between. He suggested that the size of this broad footprint seems to be increasing faster than the amount of content under encryption. Lampson added that the metadata versus content discussion is extremely problematic because the question of what information can be inferred from a given amount of metadata is not a question that theorems can be proved for, so it should be assumed that metadata will reveal a lot more information than has been thought.

---

[2] S.M. Bellovin, "What Spies Do," *SMBlog*, July 20, 2014, https://www.cs.columbia.edu/~smb/blog/2014-07/2014-07-20.html.

LaMacchia raised the concept of telemetry, that is, the data about the operation of a device in combination with its operating system and the cloud services it connects to. It is common practice for vendors—such as Microsoft, Apple, and Google, with Android phones as a key example—to collect data about how a user operates the system and to use these data to make improvements. Users have a choice of whether to opt in to this sharing of data. For example, Microsoft collects data on what causes the most common "blue screen" crashes in order to fix those problems, and data from people's browsing histories are used to help block malicious websites. These telemetry data are different from connection-oriented metadata because they are user- or system-oriented. LaMacchia suggested that future conversations could discuss the importance of telemetry, how it differs from metadata and data, and what may be detectable or deducible from the telemetry. Telemetry data should also be part of the conversation about access to data, and what types of exceptional access there should be to certain types of data. "The way we think about data that is part of the relationship between the user and service providers, for example, is getting increasingly more complex," he said, noting that labeling all these types of data as metadata glosses over categories of data that may be useful or sometimes a bad thing, in a collective environment.

Littlehale responded to the telemetry discussion by saying that telemetry represents the kind of thing that might be of value to law enforcement that it does not yet know about. Right now, the interaction between law enforcement and large service providers or large technology companies happens through a particular office that uses particular methods for the interaction. Very often, law enforcement does not know what evidence the technology company holds. "For law enforcement to accomplish its mission, we need to think about ways that we can have conversations that reveal information like this," he said. Looking at the other side, Littlehale did note the potential counterargument of service providers—that is, if users are told or if they find out that such data may be available to law enforcement, users might not choose to have this information collected.

Lampson added that he thinks of telemetry as a special case of a more general phenomenon, which is that more and more processes on a device are inextricably entangled with what goes on in the cloud. Therefore, thinking in an entirely device-centric way is going to become increasingly irrelevant for most purposes. LaMacchia agreed with this by saying that when he thinks about a device now, he thinks about a device plus services in the cloud and that combined ecosystem, of which telemetry is a part.

From the workshop panels, Kerr said he drew the conclusion that device encryption raises a distinct set of cost-benefit trade-offs and options from other forms of encryption, because, at least with current technology, the user has knowledge of the password and physical control of the devices.

CLOSING REMARKS FROM THE WORKSHOP CHAIR: TECHNOLOGY AS PART OF A SYSTEM

Cate noted the difficulty of speaking of technology in isolation, in part because everyone has their own values and convictions that are very hard to leave behind. He suggested that all stakeholders in this issue want to do the right thing, and they believe in what they are doing.

Cate also observed that technology is one part of a much bigger societal system, and it is necessary for security and public safety and other things people care about. These technologies are only a part—an important part—of the whole system, and the whole system has to work, he said.

He noted the tendency of people to think that we are on a largely fixed track, where encryption will get better and better, hacking will get better and better, and the encryption and security landscapes will look like advanced versions of today's. He cautioned that things could look vastly different in the future. For example, he suggested that fraud patterns will be different, and, extrapolating from trends of the past decade, suggested that the way in which people engage with technologies will be fundamentally different. He reemphasized the fact that technologies are not evolving in a vacuum; the societal context in which they work is also changing. He suggested that these changes could be viewed as robust progress or tremendous instability.

He also noted the importance of better educating a large segment of the population about the technologies involved in encryption and in security, suggesting that policy makers, industry leaders, judges, and others need to understand those technologies better than they do today. He noted some of the common analogies and metaphors for talking about encryption and exceptional access—for example, comparison of exceptional access to physical searches, or to providing police with keys to one's back door—suggesting that they are not always precise or accurate. Cate suggested that it could be useful for the technical people to come up with better agreed-upon, common metaphors to use when communicating about these issues.

Cate noted the importance of building trust between the technology community and law enforcement to encourage dialogue and to increase each group's understanding of how technologies are used. This, he suggested, could help make technologists' responses more appropriate, detailed, and specific. "I think we suffer not from a lack of good will, but from a trust deficit, in large part because we have a knowledge deficit," he summarized.

Cate suggested that it is hard to segregate users and uses when it comes to security. "I think that is going to be a really hard sell to say that we think the nation's secrets have to be protected, but it is okay if the public's secrets aren't so well protected," he said. However, he noted that there may be some useful ways to segregate technologies and to articulate the right technology for the right purpose.

In closing, Cate noted the exceptional collection of people who participated in the workshop: senior representatives from the FBI, senior representatives from the Office of the Director of National Intelligence, senior representatives from industry, and many of the leading lights in academia. Remarking that the workshop represented an extraordinarily important moment, he expressed his hope that it was just the beginning of a longer process.

Appendixes

A

Workshop Statement of Task

An Academies-appointed steering committee will organize a workshop addressing the use of strong encryption and implications of mechanisms for authorized government access to plaintext. The workshop will provide context on the current encryption debate and explore the implications of possible exceptional access strategies. It will specifically address the following topics: (1) encryption use cases and the feasibility of segmenting encryption policies, (2) security risks of architectures for enabling access to plaintext, and (3) technical and policy mitigations for inaccessible plaintext. The workshop will be conducted on an entirely unclassified basis and will be open to the public. A rapporteur-authored workshop summary will be prepared.

B

Workshop Agenda

WORKSHOP ON ENCRYPTION AND MECHANISMS FOR AUTHORIZED GOVERNMENT ACCESS TO PLAINTEXT

Keck Center, Washington, D.C.
June 23, 2016

9:00 a.m.	**Welcome and Opening Remarks** Fred H. Cate, Indiana University, Planning Committee Chair
Session 1.	**The Current Encryption Landscape** Fred H. Cate, Indiana University, Moderator

9:10	Panel Presentations
	    Chris Inglis, U.S. Naval Academy
	    Patrick Ball, Human Rights Data Analysis Group
	    James Baker, Federal Bureau of Investigation

10:00	Discussion
10:30	Break
Session 2.	**Encryption Use Cases and the Feasibility of Segmenting Encryption Policies** Susan Landau, Worcester Polytechnic Institute, and Frederick R. Chang, Southern Methodist University, Moderators
10:45	Kickoff Presentation Marc Donner, Uber

APPENDIX B   *51*

11:15	Discussion
12:00 p.m.	Lunch
Session 3.	**Security Risks of Architectures for Enabling Access to Plaintext** Susan Landau, Worcester Polytechnic Institute, and Frederick R. Chang, Southern Methodist University, Moderators
1:00	Kickoff Presentation Matt Blaze, University of Pennsylvania
1:30	Discussion
3:15	Break
3:45	Discussion (Continued)
4:55	Day 1 Wrap-Up
5:00	Discussion

June 24, 2016

9:00 a.m.	Welcome, Outline of Day's Goals Fred H. Cate, Steering Committee Chair
Session 4.	**Technical and Policy Mitigations for Inaccessible Plaintext** Orin Kerr, George Washington University, Moderator
9:05	Kick-off Presentation Susan Landau, Worcester Polytechnic Institute
9:35	Discussion
10:55	Break
Session 5.	**Wrap-Up** Fred H. Cate, Moderator
10:45	Reactions and Takeaways
11:30	Concluding Remarks Planning Committee
12:00 p.m.	Adjourn

C

Biographical Sketches of Workshop Planning Committee Members and Staff

FRED H. CATE, *Chair*, is a distinguished professor and the C. Ben Dutton Professor of Law at the Indiana University Maurer School of Law. He is managing director of the Center for Law, Ethics, and Applied Research in Health Information, and a senior fellow and former founding director of the Center for Applied Cybersecurity Research. Cate specializes in information privacy and security law issues. He has testified before numerous congressional committees and speaks frequently before professional, industry, and government groups. He is a senior policy advisor to the Centre for Information Policy Leadership at Hunton & Williams LLP, a member of Intel's Privacy and Security External Advisory Board, the Department of Homeland's Security Data Privacy and Integrity Committee Cybersecurity Subcommittee, the National Security Agency's (NSA's) Privacy and Civil Liberties Panel, the board of directors of The Privacy Projects, the board of directors of the International Foundation for Online Responsibility, and the board of directors of the Kinsey Institute for Research in Sex, Gender and Reproduction. Previously, Cate served as a member of the National Academies of Sciences, Engineering, and Medicine's Committee on Technical and Privacy Dimensions of Information for Terrorism Prevention, counsel to the Department of Defense Technology and Privacy Advisory Committee, reporter for the third report of the Markle Task Force on National Security in the Information Age, and a member of the Federal Trade Commission's Advisory Committee on Online Access and Security and Microsoft's Trustworthy Computing Academic Advisory Board. He chaired the International Telecommunication Union's High-Level Experts on Electronic Signatures and Certification Authorities. He served as the privacy editor for the Institute of Electrical and Electronic Engineers' *Security & Privacy* and is one of the founding editors of the journal *International Data Privacy Law*. He is the author of more than 150 books and articles, and he appears frequently in the popular press. Cate attended Oxford University and received his J.D. and his A.B. with honors and distinction from Stanford University. He is a senator and fellow (and immediate past president) of the Phi Beta Kappa Society, an elected member of the American Law Institute, and a fellow of the American Bar Foundation.

DAN BONEH is a professor of computer science and electrical engineering at Stanford University. He heads the applied cryptography group in the Computer Science department at Stanford University. Boneh's research focuses on applications of cryptography to computer security. His work includes cryptosystems with novel properties, web security, security for mobile devices, digital copyright protection, and cryptanalysis. He is a member of the National Academy of Engineering, author of more than a hundred publications in the field, and a recipient of the Packard Award, the Alfred P. Sloan Award, and the RSA award in mathematics. In 2011, Boneh received the Ishii award for industry education innovation. He received his Ph.D. from Princeton University and joined Stanford in 1997.

FREDERICK R. CHANG is the director of the Darwin Deason Institute for Cyber Security, the Bobby B. Lyle Centennial Distinguished Chair in Cyber Security, and a professor in the Department of Computer Science and Engineering at the Lyle School of Engineering of Southern Methodist University (SMU). He is also a senior fellow in the John Goodwin Tower Center for Political Studies in SMU's Dedman College and a distinguished scholar in the Robert S. Strauss Center for International Security and Law at the University of Texas, Austin. His career spans service in the private sector and in government, including as the former director of research at the NSA. Chang is a member of the National Academy of Engineering and has been awarded the NSA Director's Distinguished Service Medal.

ORIN S. KERR is the Fred C. Stevenson research professor at George Washington University Law School. He is a nationally recognized scholar of criminal procedure and computer crime law. Since he joined the faculty in 2001, his publications have been cited in more than 2,000 articles and more than 200 judicial opinions. Kerr is a former trial attorney in the Computer Crime and Intellectual Property Section at the U.S. Department of Justice, as well as a special assistant U.S. attorney in the Eastern District of Virginia. He clerked for Judge Leonard I. Garth of the U.S. Court of Appeals for the Third Circuit and Justice Anthony M. Kennedy of the U.S. Supreme Court. He has argued cases in the U.S. Supreme Court and three federal circuits. He has testified six times before congressional committees. In 2013, Chief Justice Roberts appointed Kerr to serve on the Advisory Committee for the Federal Rules of Criminal Procedure. Chief Justice Roberts appointed him again in 2015 to serve on the Judicial Conference's committee to review the Criminal Justice Act. Kerr has been a visiting professor at the University of Chicago and the University of Pennsylvania. In addition to writing more than 50 articles, he has authored and coauthored popular casebooks and coauthored the leading criminal procedure treatise. He also posts regularly at *The Washington Post*'s legal blog "The Volokh Conspiracy." The George Washington University law class of 2009 awarded Kerr the law school's teaching award. Before attending law school, he earned undergraduate and graduate degrees in mechanical engineering.

SUSAN LANDAU is professor of cybersecurity policy in the Department of Social Science and Policy Studies at Worcester Polytechnic Institute. Landau has been a senior staff privacy analyst at Google, a distinguished engineer at Sun Microsystems, and a faculty member at the University of Massachusetts, Amherst, and at Wesleyan University. She has held visiting positions at Harvard University, Cornell University, and Yale University and the Mathematical Sciences Research Institute. Landau is the author of *Surveillance or Security? The Risks Posed by New Wiretapping Technologies* (2011) and co-author with Whitfield Diffie of *Privacy on the Line: The Politics of Wiretapping and Encryption* (1998, rev. ed. 2007). She has written numerous computer science and public policy papers and op-eds on cybersecurity and encryption policy and testified before Congress on the security risks of wiretapping and on cybersecurity activities at the National Institute of Standards and Technology's Information Technology Laboratory. Landau has served on the Computer Science Telecommunications Board (CSTB) of the Academies and is currently a member of the Forum on Cyber Resilience, a roundtable of the Academies. A 2012 Guggenheim fellow, Landau was a 2010-2011 fellow at the Radcliffe Institute for Advanced Study, the recipient of the 2008 Women of Vision Social Impact Award, and also a fellow of the American Association for the Advancement of Science (AAAS) and the Association for Computing Machinery. She received her B.A. from Princeton University, her M.S. from Cornell University, and her Ph.D. from the Massachusetts Institute of Technology.

Staff

EMILY GRUMBLING is a program officer with CSTB. Since joining CSTB in 2014, Grumbling has served as study director for the Committee on Information Technology, Automation, and the U.S. Workforce, as director of the Workshop on Privacy for the Intelligence Community, and as staff to the Academies' Forum on Cyber Resilience. She previously served as an AAAS science and technology policy fellow in the Directorate for Computer and Information Science and Engineering at the National Science Foundation (2012-2014) and was an American Chemical Society (ACS) congressional fellow in the U.S. House of Representatives (2011-2012). Grumbling currently serves as a volunteer Associate of the ACS Committee on Environmental Improvement. She received her

Ph.D. in physical chemistry from the University of Arizona in 2010 and her B.A. with a double-major in chemistry and film/electronic media arts from Bard College in 2004.

ANNE FRANCES JOHNSON is founder and lead science writer at Creative Science Writing, where she provides writing and editing services for clients in academia, government, nonprofits, and industry. She previously served as a communications officer at the National Academy of Sciences. She has a master's degree in science journalism and a bachelor's in biology.

JON EISENBERG is director of CSTB. He has also been study director for a diverse body of its work, including a series of studies exploring Internet and broadband policy and networking and communications technologies. From 1995 until 1997, he was an AAAS science, engineering, and diplomacy fellow at the U.S. Agency for International Development, where he worked on technology transfer and information and telecommunications policy issues. Eisenberg received a Ph.D. in physics from the University of Washington in 1996 and a B.S. in physics with honors from the University of Massachusetts, Amherst, in 1988.

SHENAE BRADLEY is an administrative assistant at CSTB. She currently provides support for multiple projects, including Continuing Innovation in Information Technology; Information Technology, Automation, and the U.S. Workforce; and Towards 21st Century Cyber-Physical Systems Education, to name a few. Prior to this, she served as a senior project assistant with the board. Prior to coming to the Academies, she managed a number of apartment rental communities for Edgewood Management Corporation in the Maryland/D.C./Delaware metropolitan areas.

D

Biographical Sketches of Invited Workshop Participants

JAMES BAKER is general counsel for the Federal Bureau of Investigation (FBI). Most recently, he was an associate general counsel for Bridgewater Associates, LP. After clerking for the Honorable Bernard A. Friedman at the U.S. District Court for the Eastern District of Michigan, Baker joined the Department of Justice (DOJ) with the Criminal Division through the Attorney General's Honors Program in 1990 and worked as a federal prosecutor with the division's Fraud Section. In 1996, Baker joined the former Office of Intelligence Policy and Review (OIPR), which later became part of DOJ's National Security Division. From 2001 to 2007, he served as counsel for intelligence policy and head of OIPR. In this position, he developed, coordinated, and implemented national security policy with regard to intelligence and counterintelligence matters for the department. Moreover, he provided the attorney general, the U.S. intelligence community, and the White House with legal and policy advice on a range of national security issues and conducted oversight of the intelligence community, including the FBI, on behalf of the attorney general. In 2006, Baker received the George H.W. Bush Award for Excellence in counterterrorism—the Central Intelligence Agency's (CIA's) highest counterterrorism award. A year later, he received the National Security Agency's (NSA's) Intelligence Under Law Award; the NSA Director's Distinguished Service Medal; and DOJ's highest award—the Edmund J. Randolph Award. That same year, he became a fellow at the Institute of Politics at the John F. Kennedy School of Government at Harvard University and a lecturer at Harvard Law School. From 2008 to 2009, Baker was assistant general counsel for national security at Verizon Business. He then returned to DOJ, and from 2009 to 2011 served as an associate deputy attorney general working on a range of national security issues, including cybersecurity. Baker holds a juris doctorate and master's degree from the University of Michigan and is a graduate of the University of Notre Dame.

PATRICK BALL has spent 25 years designing databases and data security and conducting quantitative analysis for truth commissions, nongovernmental organizations, international criminal tribunals, and United Nations missions in El Salvador, Ethiopia, Guatemala, Haiti, South Africa, Chad, Sri Lanka, East Timor, Sierra Leone, South Africa, Kosovo, Liberia, Perú, Colombia, Iraq, the Democratic Republic of Congo, and Syria. From 1993 to 2003, he worked in several capacities in the Science and Human Rights Program at the American Association for the Advancement of Science, where he began recruiting colleagues to build the Human Rights Data Analysis Group (HRDAG). From 2003 to 2013 he continued to develop HRDAG from within Benetech, a nonprofit technology company in Silicon Valley. While at Benetech, he designed Martus, a self-encrypting, self-replicating, open-source database for human rights projects. From 2013 through 2015, he was executive director of HRDAG; since December 2015, he has been

HRDAG's director of research. He provided testimony in two cases at the International Criminal Tribunal for the former Yugoslavia, the first in the trial of Slobodan Milošević, the former president of Serbia, and he has advised the Special Court in Sierra Leone and the International Criminal Court. In 2013, he provided expert testimony in Guatemala's Supreme Court in the trial of General José Efraín Ríos Montt, the de-facto president of Guatemala in 1982-1983. Ríos was found guilty of genocide and crimes against humanity; it was the first time ever that a former head of state was found guilty of genocide in his own country. In September 2015, Ball provided expert testimony in the trial of former president of Chad, Hissène Habré. In June 2014, the American Statistical Association honored Ball as a fellow. In April 2005, the Electronic Frontier Foundation (EFF) named Ball a Pioneer of the Electronic Frontier. In June 2004, the Association for Computing Machinery (ACM) gave him the Eugene Lawler Award for Humanitarian Contributions within Computer Science and Informatics, and in 2002, he received a Special Achievement Award from the Social Statistics Section of the American Statistical Association. He is a fellow at the Center for Human Rights Science at Carnegie Mellon University, at the Human Rights Center of the Boalt School of Law at the University of California, Berkeley, and in the Department of Government at Essex University, and he is on the technical advisory board of AccessNow. He has been profiled in *The New York Times Magazine*, *Wired*, *Foreign Policy*, *Salon.com*, and the *Christian Science Monitor*, and he has been featured in a PBS film. Ball received his B.A. degree from Columbia University and his Ph.D. from the University of Michigan.

KEVIN BANKSTON is the director of New America's Open Technology Institute (OTI), where he works in the public interest to promote policy and regulatory reforms to strengthen communities by supporting open communications networks, platforms, and technologies. He previously served as OTI's policy director. Prior to leading OTI's policy team, Bankston was a senior counsel and the director of the Free Expression Project at the Center for Democracy and Technology (CDT), a Washington, D.C.-based nonprofit organization dedicated to promoting democratic values and constitutional liberties in the digital age. From that position, he spent 2 years advocating on a wide range of Internet and technology policy issues both international and domestic, most recently organizing a broad coalition of companies and civil society organizations to demand greater transparency around the U.S. government's surveillance practices. He also has served since 2005 on the board of the First Amendment Coalition, a nonprofit public-interest organization dedicated to advancing free speech and a more open and accountable government, and previously was a nonresidential fellow at the Stanford Law School's Center for Internet and Society. Prior to joining CDT, Bankston worked for nearly a decade at the EFF, specializing in free speech and privacy law with a focus on government surveillance, Internet privacy, and location privacy. As a senior staff attorney at EFF, he regularly litigated issues surrounding free expression and electronic surveillance and was a lead counsel in EFF's lawsuits against the NSA and AT&T, challenging the legality of the NSA warrantless wiretapping program, first revealed in 2005. Bankston originally joined EFF as an Equal Justice Works/Bruce J. Ennis First Amendment Fellow, studying the impact of post-9/11 antiterrorism surveillance initiatives on online privacy and free expression. Before joining EFF, he litigated Internet-related free speech cases at the national office of the American Civil Liberties Union in New York City as a Justice William Brennan First Amendment Fellow. He received his J.D. at the University of Southern California Law School after receiving his B.A. at the University of Texas, Austin.

MATT BLAZE is an associate professor of computer and information science at the University of Pennsylvania. His research focuses on focuses on cryptography and its applications, trust management, human scale security, secure systems design, and networking and distributed computing. He is particularly interested in security technology with bearing on public policy issues, including cryptography policy (key escrow), wiretapping and surveillance, and the security of electronic voting systems. He was also a veteran of the first crypto wars in the 1990s. He discovered a serious flaw in the U.S. government's Clipper encryption system in 1994, which had been proposed as a mechanism for the public to encrypt their data in a way that would still allow access by law enforcement. He edited several influential reports on encryption policy, including the 1998 study of key escrow systems that demonstrated that such systems are inherently less secure and more expensive than systems without such a feature. Blaze's work contributed to the recent shift in U.S. encryption policy, and he is a leader in the current debate. He has testified before various committees of the U.S. Congress and European Parliament on this issue several times. He received his Ph.D. in computer science from Princeton University.

APPENDIX D
57

JAMES BURRELL serves as a senior federal government executive in the position of deputy assistant director at the FBI. His current responsibilities include executive leadership for agencywide research, development, and advancement of applied technologies for investigative and intelligence operations. In this position, he also directed global FBI cyber investigative and intelligence operations to counter current and emerging cyberthreats impacting the United States. He has extensive diplomatic and national policy experience as a delegate to multinational organizations and as a senior representative to interagency governmental and national security policy committees. Burrell has academic affiliations as a faculty member and research advisor for graduate-level computer science and engineering programs at public and private universities. He earned B.S., M.S., Ed.S., and Ph.D. degrees in the fields of electrical engineering and computer and information sciences. He also received professional and technical certifications in information technology, information security, and digital forensic science. He is recognized as a senior member of the Institute of Electrical and Electronics Engineers (IEEE), a professional member of the ACM, and an inductee to the Upsilon Pi Epsilon International Honor Society.

MARC DONNER is the engineering site director for Uber in New York City. Donner's research career includes time at NASA's Jet Propulsion Laboratory where he worked on planetary radar, and at IBM Research, where he worked on ultrahigh-resolution displays, real-time systems, robotics, and distributed computing. His industrial career includes work with Morgan Stanley, Union Bank of Switzerland, Google, and MSCI. Donner's professional interests cover a broad range of technical areas, including cybersecurity, privacy, software engineering, distributed computing, quantitative finance, robotics, and system administration. He is active in the Usenix Association, IEEE, and the ACM. He contributes his time pro bono to a number of charitable, nonprofit, and public service organizations, often by serving as their webmaster. His blog may be found at nygeek.wordpress.com. He received a B.S. in electrical engineering from the California Institute of Technology and a Ph.D. in computer science (robotics) from Carnegie Mellon University.

MATT GREEN is an assistant professor at the Johns Hopkins Information Security Institute. His research includes techniques for privacy-enhanced information storage, anonymous payment systems, and bilinear map-based cryptography. He was formerly a partner in Independent Security Evaluators, a custom security evaluation and design consultancy, and he currently consults independently. Green's research focus is in the area of applied cryptography. His recent work includes developing privacy-preserving cryptographic protocols for implementing anonymous electronic cash and identification. He has also developed protocols that allow users to access databases without revealing which data they are accessing. Additionally, Green has been working on new automation techniques to assist in the design and deployment of advanced cryptographic protocols. He also works in the area of cryptographic engineering. This work involves understanding the practical aspects of cryptographic systems, implementing cryptographic protocols, and in some cases reverse-engineering deployed systems. He also teaches an introductory course on this subject. Additionally, Green has designed several cryptographic tools, including Charm, a framework for rapidly prototyping cryptosystems, and a functional encryption library that provides implementations of several new Attribute Based Encryption schemes. From 1999 to 2003, Green served as a senior technical staff member at AT&T Laboratories/Research in Florham Park, New Jersey. He has a Ph.D. in computer science from Johns Hopkins University.

DANIEL KAHN GILLMOR is a senior staff technologist for the American Civil Liberties Union's Speech, Privacy, and Technology project, focused on the way technical infrastructure shapes society and impacts civil liberties. As a free software developer and member of the Debian project, he contributes to fundamental tools that shape the possibilities of our information-rich environment. As a participant in the Internet Engineering Task Force (IETF), he fosters the creation of new generations of networking and cryptographic protocols designed and optimized for privacy and security. Gillmor is an antisurveillance advocate for privacy, justice, free speech, and data sovereignty. He is a graduate of Brown University's computer science program.

CHRIS INGLIS retired from the Department of Defense in January 2014 following more than 41 years of federal service, including 28 years at NSA and seven and a half years as its senior civilian and deputy director. He began his career at NSA as a computer scientist within the National Computer Security Center, followed by tours in information assurance, policy, time-sensitive operations, and signals intelligence organizations. Promoted to NSA's Senior Executive Service in 1997, he held a variety of senior leadership assignments and twice served away from NSA Headquarters, first as a visiting professor of computer science at the U.S. Military Academy (1991-1992) and later as the U.S. Special Liaison to the United Kingdom (2003-2006). Inglis holds advanced degrees in engineering and computer science from Columbia University (M.S.), Johns Hopkins University (M.S.), and George Washington University (professional degree). He is also a graduate of the Kellogg Business School executive development program, the U.S. Air Force (USAF) Air War College, the Air Command and Staff College, and the Squadron Officers' School. Inglis' military career includes over 30 years of service in the USAF—9 years on active duty and 21 years in the Air National Guard—from which he retired as a brigadier general in 2006. He holds the rating of Command Pilot and commanded units at the squadron, group, and joint force headquarters levels. Inglis' significant awards include the Clements award as the U.S. Naval Academy's Outstanding Military Faculty member (1984), three Presidential Rank Awards (2000, 2004, 2009), the USAF Distinguished Service Medal (2006), the Boy Scouts of America Distinguished Eagle Scout Award (2009), the Director of National Intelligence Distinguished Service Medal (2014), and the President's National Security Medal (2014).

BRIAN LAMACCHIA is the director of the Security and Cryptography group within Microsoft Research (MSR) where his team conducts basic and applied research and advanced development. He is also a founding member of the Microsoft Cryptography Review Board and consults on security and cryptography architectures, protocols and implementations across the company. Before moving into MSR in 2009, he was the architect for cryptography in Windows Security, development lead for .NET Framework Security and program manager for core cryptography in Windows 2000. Prior to joining Microsoft, he was a member of the Public Policy Research Group at AT&T Labs—Research. In addition to his responsibilities at Microsoft, LaMacchia is an adjunct associate professor in the School of Informatics and Computing at Indiana University-Bloomington and an affiliate faculty member of the Department of Computer Science and Engineering at the University of Washington. He also currently serves as president of the board of directors of the Seattle International Film Festival, general chair of Crypto 2016, and as an ex officio member of the board of directors of the International Association for Cryptologic Research. He received S.B., S.M., and Ph.D. degrees in electrical engineering and computer science from the Massachusetts Institute of Technology (MIT) in 1990, 1991, and 1996, respectively.

BUTLER LAMPSON is a technical fellow at Microsoft Corporation and an adjunct professor of computer science and electrical engineering at MIT. He was on the faculty at Berkeley and then at the Computer Science Laboratory at Xerox PARC and at Digital's Systems Research Center. He has worked on computer architecture, local area networks, raster printers, page description languages, operating systems, remote procedure call, programming languages and their semantics, programming in the large, fault-tolerant computing, transaction processing, computer security, WYSIWYG editors, and tablet computers. Lampson was one of the designers of the SDS 940 time-sharing system, the Alto personal distributed computing system, the Xerox 9700 laser printer, two-phase commit protocols, the Autonet LAN, the SDSI/SPKI system for network security, the Microsoft Tablet PC software, the Microsoft Palladium high-assurance stack, and several programming languages. He holds a number of patents on networks, security, raster printing, and transaction processing. He is a member of the National Academy of Sciences and the National Academy of Engineering and a fellow of the ACM and the American Academy of Arts and Sciences. He received the ACM Software Systems Award in 1984 for his work on the Alto, the IEEE Computer Pioneer award in 1996, the National Computer Systems Security Award in 1998, the IEEE von Neumann Medal in 2001, the Turing Award in 1992, and the National Academy of Engineering's Draper Prize in 2004. At Microsoft Lampson has worked on anti-piracy, security, fault-tolerance, and user interfaces. He was one of the designers of Palladium, and he spent 2 years as an architect in the Tablet PC group. Currently he is in Microsoft Research, working on security, privacy, and fault-tolerance, and kibitzing in systems, networking, and other areas. He received an A.B. from Harvard University, a Ph.D. in electrical engineering and computer science from the University of California, Berkeley, and honorary Sc.D. degrees from the Eidgenössische Technische Hochschule, Zurich, and the University of Bologna.

APPENDIX D

RICHARD LITTLEHALE is assistant special agent in charge of the Tennessee Bureau of Investigation's Technical Services Unit, which includes TBI's electronic surveillance, digital forensics, online child exploitation, and cyber investigation functions. He has testified as an expert witness in the law enforcement use of communications records in numerous homicide and violent crime trials. Littlehale is an attorney, and serves as one of TBI's primary constitutional law and criminal procedure trainers. He has provided instruction to law enforcement officers at all levels of government in techniques for obtaining and using communications evidence in support of criminal investigations, and is active in national groups of law enforcement technical and electronic surveillance specialists, including the National Technical Investigators Association and the FBI Law Enforcement Technical Forum. He serves as a subject-matter expert on electronic surveillance for the Association of State Criminal Investigative Agencies and the International Association of Chiefs of Police. In that capacity, he represents the law enforcement community's interest in lawful access to communications evidence at the national level before Congress and other groups. He received his bachelor's degree in 1992 from Bowdoin College and his law degree in 1995 from Vanderbilt Law School.

ERIC RESCORLA is a fellow in the office of the chief technology officer at Mozilla, focused on developing the next generation of internet technologies for networking, security, and real-time media. Since joining Mozilla in 2013, he has been focused on advanced technologies and Mozilla's technical strategy. He was instrumental in the development of WebRTC, which brought voice and video to the browser and worked with Cisco to start OpenH264, which allows Open Source projects to use the world's most popular video codec for free. He also played a key role in starting Let's Encrypt, which makes it easy for anyone to run a secure website. Rescorla's background is in communications security, especially Transport Layer Security (TLS), the foundational security protocol for the Web. He is the former chair of the IETF TLS working group as well as the editor of the TLS and HTTPS specification. He co-designed DTLS, and he is the author of one of the standard books on TLS. He was on the Internet Architecture Board from 2002 to 2008 and in 2007 served on California Secretary of State Debra Bowen's Top-to-Bottom Review of the voting systems certified for use in California. Rescorla holds a B.S. in chemistry from Yale University.

ANDREW SHERMAN heads the security practice at Eden Technologies, a New York City-based information technology consultancy, where he has worked with clients in financial services, health care, and local government. After starting his private-sector career at AT&T Bell Laboratories, he moved into the financial industry. For nearly 20 years, he has focused exclusively on information security, primarily in financial services. He has a strong interest in data security, data governance, and privacy as well as related identity and access management issues. A graduate of Vassar College, Sherman has a Ph.D. in physics from Rensselaer Polytechnic Institute and additional research experience in machine vision and pattern recognition.

GUY "BUD" TRIBBLE is vice president of software technology at Apple, Inc. Tribble began his career at Apple where, as manager of the original Macintosh software team, he helped to design the Mac OS and user interface. He joined Apple from Eazel, Inc., where he was vice president of engineering, leading development of next-generation user interface software and Internet services for Linux computers. Before that, Tribble was chief technology officer for the Sun-Netscape Alliance, responsible for guiding Internet and e-commerce software research and development. He also helped found NeXT Computer, where he was vice president of Software Engineering and a key architect of the NextStep operating system. Tribble earned a B.A. degree in physics at the University of California, San Diego, and an M.D. and a Ph.D. in biophysics and physiology at the University of Washington, Seattle.

E

Acronyms and Abbreviations

ACLU	American Civil Liberties Union
CALEA	Communications Assistance for Law Enforcement Act
CSTB	Computer Science and Telecommunications Board
DEA	Drug Enforcement Agency
DNS	Domain Name System
FBI	Federal Bureau of Investigation
HRDAG	Human Rights Data Analysis Group
IoT	Internet of Things
ISIL/ISIS	Islamic State of Iraq and the Levant/Islamic State of Iraq and Syria, otherwise referred to as the Islamic State
NSA	National Security Agency
ODNI	Office of the Director of National Intelligence
SSL	Secure Sockets Layer
TBI	Tennessee Bureau of Investigation
TLS	Transport Layer Security
TSD-3600	Telephone Secure Device-3600
VEP	Vulnerabilities Equities Process